COL

MOSCOW 1 ...GRAD KIEV

Collets Guide
to
MOSCOW   LENINGRAD
KIEV

3-day visits to each city

---

by

JENNIFER and VICTOR LOUIS

Collets

First published in 1990 by
Collets Holdings Ltd
Denington Estate, Wellingborough, Northants
Great Britain

ISBN 0 569 09028 8

A CIP catalogue record for this book
is available from the British Library

Photoset in North Wales by
Derek Doyle & Associates, Mold, Clwyd
Printed and bound in Great Britain by
Biddles Limited, Guildford, Surrey

Contents

List of Illustrations   7

Brief History of Moscow and the Soviet Union   9

MOSCOW

Day 1   Kremlin, Red Square, Bolshoi Theatre ...   35
Day 2   Novodevichy Convent, GUM, boat trip ...   61
Day 3   A palace, Beryozka shop, Puppet Theatre ...   69
Useful Information   77
Map   78
Cooperative Restaurants   85

LENINGRAD

Day 1   Hermitage, Kirov Ballet ...   100
Day 2   Nevsky Prospect, boat trip ...   105
Day 3   Petrodvorets, White Nights ...   115
Map   124
Useful Information   127

KIEV

Day 1   City tour ...   139
Day 2   St Sophia's, Folk Art Museum ...   145
Day 3   Above the Dnieper, Art Gallery,
        Babi Yar ...   149
Useful Information   154
Map   156

Illustrations

MOSCOW

following page 27

1 The Arbat
2 Red Square
3 St Basil's Cathedral
4 The Kremlin
5 Rossia Hotel and Old Churches
6 The River
7 The Pushkin Statue

LENINGRAD

following page 89

8 The River Neva
9 The Old Stock Exchange Building
10 Peter and Paul Cathedral
11 The Mint
12 The Admiralty Spire
13 Alexander's Column
14 Embankment of the Neva
15 The Winter Palace (Hermitage)
16 Nevsky Prospect

KIEV

following page 131

17 Andreyevsky Hill
18 St Sophia's Cathedral
19 Monastery of the Caves
20 Fountains on Kiev Square
21 Khmelnitsky's Statue
22 St Andrew's Church

A Brief History of Russia and the Soviet Union
as reflected in the cities of Kiev Moscow and Leningrad

The history of the Soviet Union follows the ups and downs of her three largest cities, each of them deserving the status of capital – ancient Kiev (now the capital of the Ukraine), Moscow (now capital of the country for the second time) and Leningrad, which Peter the Great built as his capital city of St. Petersburg, to his own magnificent plan.

**The Waterways
**Ki and Kiev State
**Rurik

In the earliest times of which there is any record of the northern part of Russia, the River Neva served as an artery of trade between Europe and Asia; according to Arabian and Persian chronicles, the Persians and even the Hindus received goods from the West along this route. It was the starting-point of the great waterways running from the Varangians to the Greeks, through the Volkhov and the Dnieper rivers, and from the Varangians to the Arabs along the Volga. Saxon and Arabian coins dug up in several places at the mouth of the Neva and on the shores of Lake Ladoga provide evidence of this ancient traffic. Nestor, the 11th-century Russian chronicler, recorded that 'The Neva served as a means of communication between peoples of the West and Novgorod through the Volkhov; by the Neva they went into the Varangian Sea, and by that sea to Rome.'

But Nestor wrote seven hundred years before St. Petersburg was founded, so our story begins with Kiev. Kiev took its name from the first prince of the Slav tribe, the Polyane, who lived far to the south. He was called Ki, and with his brothers he founded the town at the end of the 5th century. By the year 800 the Kievan state was firmly established. The state of Novgorod grew in the north, and in 862 Norsemen, led by the Vikings Rurik, Sineus and Truvor, were invited by the Novgorod Republic to come and restore order. One of these, Rurik, became the first of the Rurikids to rule in Russia, their reign lasted until the end of the 16th century. In 882 Oleg, Rurik's successor in Novgorod, conquered Kiev and thus united the two states and introduced a period of prosperity for them both.

**Kiev town

Kiev's early development was unusual, mainly due to

its hilly site. It consisted of three separate settlements. The Upper City (Staro-Kiev) which overlooked the Podol, meaning 'low', was the trading area close to the Dnieper. The third settlement was also on high ground above the river, but set at some distance behind Staro-Kiev; this was Pechersk, where vast natural caves are to be found. Hermits lived in them until the Monastery of the Caves was founded. In spite of its divided layout, Kiev was strong enough to become the capital of the country.

It was also the trading centre of Eastern Europe, and had trading relations with the countries of Western Europe and the Baltic as well as Armenia, Constantinople and Arabia. Its importance gave rise to a Russian proverb, reminiscent of 'All roads lead to Rome', saying 'Your tongue will lead you to Kiev', meaning you had but to ask the way.

**Prince Vladimir
**Christianity

But it is in the reign of Prince Vladimir (978–1015) that the Golden Age of Kiev begins. In 988 Prince Vladimir introduced Christianity into Russia. According to chronicles he was a violent man, 'insatiable in vice' and a fanatical heathen who had offered thousands of human sacrifices. His shrewdness is evident from the legendary account of his quest for a new religion. Vladimir, the legend runs, considered many religions before finally choosing Christianity. The Jewish faith was admirable, but the thought that its followers had been scattered throughout the earth for their sins distressed him. Islam he rejected on the grounds that total abstinence was incompatible with survival in a cold climate. Roman Catholicism he could not accept because he himself would have become subservient to the Pope. The emissaries Prince Vladimir sent to find out about the Greek Orthodox

Church reported on their return, 'The Greeks led us to the edifices where they worship their God; and we knew not whether we were in heaven or on earth. For on earth there is no such splendour or beauty, and we are at a loss how to describe it. We only know that God dwells there among men, and their service is fairer than the ceremonies of other nations. We can never forget that beauty.' Accordingly, Vladimir was baptized, married to Princess Anna, sister of the Greek Emperor, and adopted Christianity as the religion for the country as a whole. Mass baptism took place in the Dnieper even though it was mid-winter, and Prince Vladimir was canonised for his part in the conversions.

**Russian Orthodoxy

This would seem a good moment to say more about the Russian Orthodox Church. Its pride is that it has survived, unchanged, since those early years. It is a branch of the Eastern Orthodox Church, the second largest body of organised Christians in the world, consisting of a number of independent and self-governing Churches, among them the Churches of Russia and Georgia and the autonomous Churches of Estonia and Latvia which are also independent, except that the appointment of their chief bishops requires the sanction of their Mother Church, the Church of Russia.

When Russia adopted Orthodoxy in 988–998, the religion had already a thousand years' experience behind it, and so the books, the doctrine, the music and paintings, the monastic system and even the architectural style were taken over as they stood, in working order so to speak. They were regarded as an integrated whole, already as perfect as may be as the name 'Orthodox' even then conveyed; it means 'that which guards and teaches the right belief' and admits of no alteration. The rigidity and conservatism of the

Russian Church was intensified by centuries of threat from enemies with other faiths. The only change was the translation of the Greek texts into Old Slavonic. As the Russian Church spread, so the Arabian and Tatar peoples had translations made for them and the peoples of the north and right across Siberia were provided for in their turn.

**Church architecture

Naturally, different parts of the country and different stages in the history of the Soviet Union have produced variations of the form of ecclesiastical architecture, but it is still safe to say that most Russian churches are built on a rectangular plan and have five domes, with the largest in the middle. Ancient Russia was a land of wooden buildings, prone to devastating fires and often the local church of brick or stone is all that remains of the past. If the church is in a good state of preservation the domes may be gilded, painted silver or some bright colour, and surmounted by a Greek cross. The belfry, which has no clock, is generally a separate structure standing nearby.

**Church interiors

Inside the church the sanctuary is separated from the main body of the building by the iconostasis, a screen with sacred pictures (icons) on it. The icons may be richly framed and decorated, and have a lamp burning before them. Slender wax candles, which are on sale in the church, are also placed before them by the faithful. Of the three doors leading through the inconostasis, the central one, known as the Holy Door, is used by priests only. The language used during the services is Church Slavonic.

There are no seats in the church and even though the services are long the congregation remains standing. The very ordeal is an act of worship. If, as a visitor, you get tired feet you will not be the first to complain. In 1656 the Archdeacon of Aleppo wrote, 'As for the Muscovites, their feet must surely be of iron'. The singing, which is always unaccompanied but in which the congregation readily joins, is led by the choir, dressed in ordinary clothes and usually standing out of sight. By contrast the rich vestments of the priests provide another link with the distant past, having been taken directly from the clothing once worn at the court of Byzantium.

The head of the Church is the Patriarch of Moscow and All Russia, and the bishops of Moscow, Leningrad, Kiev, Minsk and Novosibirsk bear the title of Metropolitan.

**Church & State

Although the Russian Orthodox Church is quite separate from the Soviet State, a government council has been set up to maintain relations between the state and the religious bodies. This is the Council for Religious Affairs which has its headquarters in Moscow.

**Names of churches

The following are among the more usual names of churches in Russia. Tserkov or Khram means church; Sobor means Cathedral:

Church of ...

the Annunciation	Blagoveshchenskaya
the Epiphany	Bogoyavlenskaya
the Transfiguration	Preobrazhenskaya
the Elevation of the Cross	Krestodvizhenskaya or Vozdvizhenskaya
the Deposition of the Robe	Rizopolozheniya
the Resurrection	Voskresenskaya
the Ascension	Voznesenskaya

the Nativity of the Virgin	Rozhdestvo Bogoroditsi
the Immaculate Conception	Zachatyevskaya
the Presentation of the Virgin	Vvedeniya
the Purification of the Virgin	Sreteniya
the Apparition of the Virgin	Znamenskaya
the Intercession of the Virgin	Pokrovskaya
Our Lady of All Sorrows	Skorbyashchenskaya
the Assumption	Uspenskaya
the Holy Trinity	Troitskaya

Very many churches are also dedicated to favourite saints, and those to St. Nicholas, SS. Peter and Paul, St. George, SS. Boris and Gleb, St. Vladimir, St. Dmitri, SS. Cosmo and Demian, and St. Sergei are easily recognisable from their Russian names.

More difficult are St. John the Baptist (Ioann Predtecha) and the prophet Elijah (Ilya Prorok).

**Rival city-states
**Foundation of Moscow

The acceptance of Christianity brought Kiev into closer contact with Byzantium, and the adoption of the autocratic government as well as the architecture of Constantinople. There were, however, many city-states besides Kiev, and constant wars raged between them. The official date for the founding of Moscow is accepted as 1147. Prince Yuri Dolgoruky of Rostov-Suzdal, who had founded Moscow as a southern border settlement, wrote to his friend Prince Svyatoslav inviting him to Moscow to attend a banquet in honour of Prince Chernigov saying, 'Come to me, brother, in Moscow'. The fortress was surrounded by a strong wooden fence but it was small and of little consequence.

**Beginning of the decline of Kiev
**Vladimir as capital
**Genghis-Khan and the Mongol-Tatar raids

After its early period of glory Kiev began to decline in importance, partly due to family strife. In 1169 Prince Andrei of Vladimir conquered it, and proclaimed Vladimir (800 km/500 miles to the north-east) the new capital. In 1224 Russia suffered her first encounter with the advance army of Genghis Khan, and this was followed by the Tatar invasions. From 1237–1242 the Tatars under Batu Khan conquered Russia and established in the Volga steppes the rule of the Golden Horde to which all Russia became vassal and paid tribute.

**Rise of Moscow

In 1238 the Moscow fortress was burnt down by the invaders, but during the rule of the Golden Horde Moscow actually grew in prosperity in spite of its vassal state. The princes of Moscow acted as tax-collectors for the Tatars and even used Tatar soldiers in their campaigns against neighbouring principalities. Ivan I, known as Ivan Kalita (Ivan Money-Bags) for the way he accumulated treasure, became the first Grand Duke of Moscow in 1328. A few years earlier the Metropolitan of the Church had moved his seat to Moscow from the old church capital of Vladimir, an act which added to the already growing importance of the city.

**Dmitri Donskoy
**Tamerlane

In 1380 Dmitri Donskoy (Demetrius of the Don), Grand-Prince of Muscovy, won an important battle against the Tatars. The Grand-Princedom of Muscovy had by this time obtained power over most of the older principalities by its tax-collecting. Although Dmitri

Donskoy's battle was not decisive, the Tatar grip on the country was considerably loosened, but even so their dreaded raids continued. In 1395, when it seemed that nothing would halt a new advance by Tamerlane, the tsar commanded that the treasured icon of Our Lady of Vladimir be brought to Moscow. It had scarcely arrived when news was brought that Tamerlane had ordered a retreat. The icon remained in the new capital.

**Ivan III
**Moscow's supremacy
**Ivan the Great

After the fall of Constantinople in 1453 a Pskov monk wrote that 'Two Romes have already fallen, but the third remains standing and a fourth there will not be' and Moscow became known as the Third Rome. This occurred during the reign of Ivan III of Muscovy (1462–1505), also known as Ivan the Great. Ivan married Sophia, niece of the last Byzantine Emperor, considered himself heir to the Byzantine Empire and adopted their double-headed eagle which remained the arms of the Russian Empire until 1917. It had been the policy of the early princes of Muscovy to gain control of the waterways with an outlet to the sea by conquering the neighbouring principalities. Ivan laid the foundations of the future Russian empire when, between 1465 and 1488, he annexed the rich, strong city of Novgorod with its vast territories, defied the Tatars by refusing to pay them further taxes and routed the Golden Horde's armies sent against him. It ended 250 years of Tatar oppression.

**The Kremlin

During the reign of Ivan III the first stone and brick buildings of the Moscow Kremlin were built, including the walls and the Cathedrals of the Assumption and Annunciation. They were built by foreign architects, mostly from northern Italy, who were all given the surname of Friasine, meaning Franc, but with workmen bringing influences from the Russian towns of Vladimir, Pskov and Novgorod. In this way the original form of Moscow architecture developed.

**Ivan the Terrible
**Growth of Muscovy

Although he came to the throne in 1533, it was only in 1547 that Ivan IV (known as the Terrible) was crowned in Moscow with the royal diadem and assumed the title of Tsar (the word is derived from 'caesar') of All the Russias. Ivan IV built a powerful and united Russian state; during his reign the last of the other independent principalities disappeared from the map of Russia. He received his nickname for his severe persecution of the 'boyars' (barons) who had possessed great influence in government. The tsar's power became absolute and Ivan increased the crown lands by confiscation, as had Henry VIII of England. Territorial gains from nearby principalities, Novgorod's collapse in 1570 when the tsar is said to have massacred 60,000 Novgorodians, and the opening of the trade route to Western Europe from the White Sea in the 16th century, all increased Moscow's importance. In 1552 and 1557 the Tatar kingdoms of Kazan and Astrakhan were conquered. In 1582 the Russian conquest of Siberia began. Moscow became an important point on the Baltic-Volga-Caspian trade route by which goods were transported from the south to the Baltic and thence to Europe, but although its prosperity continued to grow, the city was periodically raided by the Tatars until 1591.

**Time of Troubles
**Minin and Pozharsky

Ivan the Terrible died in 1584. When Feodor I, Ivan's

son, died in 1598, ending the Rurik dynasty, 15 years of turmoil followed. He was succeeded by his brother-in-law, Boris Godunov, who died mysteriously in 1605. Boris Godunov had been opposed by two false Dmitris, each claiming in turn to be Dmitri, Ivan the Terrible's youngest son who had died in 1591. Both impostors were supported by the Poles. Organised government collapsed and a disastrous civil war ensued. At one point the Poles were near to the Kremlin, but they were driven from the country in 1613 by an army of volunteers led by a meat merchant, Kosma Minin, and Prince Pozharsky (whose statue stands in Red Square). In the same year the first of the Romanovs, Mikhail Romanov, was elected tsar by the Land Assembly (Zemsky Sobor) in Moscow. In spite of the troublous times, the growth of Moscow continued almost uninterrupted.

**Kiev's final decline
**Ukrainian independence

Kiev had been suffering her own troubles during this period. A series of fires devastated the city during the 12th century, and in 1240 it was plundered by the Tatars. An Italian traveller who visited Kiev six years later wrote that most of the churches had been burnt and that only 200 houses remained. After the Tatar invasion and the decline of the Kiev State the area now known as the Ukraine changed masters several times, being held by Russia and Poland. Then it was devastated by the Crimean Tatars. It was under Lithuanian rule from 1320 to 1455. In the 16th century Ukrainian hatred of the Polish landlords increased as they took the most fertile land for themselves and tried to introduce Catholicism. In 1654 the Cossacks, the most militarist people of the Ukrainian population at the time, led by Hetman (Cossack military leader) Bogdan Khmelnitsky, won independence from Poland

and established a state of their own in the central part of the present-day Ukraine. Then, as the new state could not possibly survive alone, it chose to unite with Muscovy, the agreement proclaiming that they 'should be one for ever', adding further to Moscow's dominance.

**Kiev's revival

Kiev then became a city of merchants, and many magnificent buildings were erected in the 17th and 18th centuries, many in baroque style. The city spread along the river and its three original settlements were quickly surrounded by houses and other buildings.

**Peter the Great
**Foundation of St. Petersburg

Peter I (the Great) came to the throne in 1682. Until 1696 he ruled jointly with his brother, Ivan V; he then became sole ruler of Russia. Peter I was one of the most outstanding statesmen and warriors in Russian history. Rightly called the 'enlightener of Russia', he introduced Western customs, culture and technical achievements into his backward country. He extended Russian domination to the southern shore of the Caspian Sea, won access to the Baltic, reorganised the national economy, founded a new army and Russia's first large fleet. But his greatest memorial remains the spacious city he founded in 1703, originally named St. Petersburg after its founder (and still affectionately called 'Peter' by its inhabitants). The city's growth conformed to strict geometrical planning under the personal direction of Peter I. It was proclaimed the new capital in 1712.

**Moscow 'plays second fiddle'

Moscow had the status of Russia's second capital. Pushkin wrote:

And Moscow bowed to the new capital

As the Queen Dowager bows to the young Queen ...

Moscow lost much of its former glory and an order of Peter the Great in 1714, when he was concerned at the shortage of masons to work on his new capital, forbade any further building in stone except in St. Petersburg, reducing Moscow's status still further. Even during this period, however, a few fine buildings were erected which, although of wood, were given the appearance of stone by a stucco finish on the wood.

Peter's successors preferred the old capital. During the reigns of Elizaveta Petrovna, daughter of Peter I (1741–1761) and of Catherine II (the Great) (1762–1796) some of the finest houses in Moscow were built. Besides these, several large estates such as Arkhangelskoye, Kuskovo and Ostankino were built outside the city.

**Catherine the Great

Catherine's reign is notable for the extension of Russian territory after the three partitions of Poland, for victorious wars with Turkey and for the acquisition of the Crimean and Danubian principalities. During this period Russia became a Great Power. Catherine II was succeeded by her son, Paul I (1796–1801), unpopular with the nobility and eventually assassinated in his palace.

**Napoleon

He was succeeded by his son, Alexander I (1801–1825), founder of the Holy Alliance and principal figure in the coalition that defeated Napoleon. Napoleon invaded Russia in 1812 with disastrous consequences for himself. The fire which ravaged Moscow for three days and nights is well known. When the French troops were forced to evacuate the city, three quarters of the houses had been destroyed by fire but an order to blow up the Kremlin on departure was only partially carried out. Over a quarter of the 100,000 men of the Grande Armée who had entered Moscow had been taken prisoner or died from hunger. The following year the reconstruction of the city began, and it was completed by a special commission set up by the tsar in 1825. Most of the new building was in brick and whole new streets appeared. After the defeat of Napoleon, Alexander I became the most powerful sovereign in Europe, and during his reign Georgia, Azerbaijan, Bessarabia, Finland and Poland were added to the Russian Empire.

**The Decembrists

Nicholas I (1825–1855) followed his brother. During the short interregnum caused by Alexander I's sudden death, a group of aristocratic officers made the first military attempt to overthrow the autocracy of the tsars, and to change the system of serfdom. This rebellion took place on the 14 December 1825, and the rebels were accordingly known as the Decembrists. The uprising was promptly suppressed, and its leaders were hanged or sent to Siberia; but it nevertheless gave powerful impetus to the further development of liberal thought in Russia, although its immediate effect was to produce a period of intense persecution and an affirmation of the autocratic powers of Tsar Nicholas.

Alexander II (1855–1881) was the son of Nicholas. In 1861 he issued a decree for the emancipation of the serfs, making possible industrial expansion. The Caucasus was conquered and in 1877–1878 the war with Turkey was won, resulting in independence for Bulgaria.

During the last half of the 19th century the population of Moscow grew rapidly: from 350,000 in 1863 to 1,039,000 in 1879. Moscow had been an important trade and craft centre since the Middle Ages and was affected more than other Russian towns by industrialisation and the industrial boom of the 1890s. By the eve of the revolution Moscow had become the financial, commercial and industrial capital of Russia.

Kiev also grew and prospered in the 19th century particularly when it was elevated to the status of provincial centre. The city's growth was temporarily halted by a series of fires, the most disastrous of which was in 1811. It raged for several days and Podol, the most densely inhabited part of Kiev, suffered badly. General reconstruction of the city began in May 1812, and by the middle of the century the central part had wide, well-planned streets with many attractive buildings. Kiev became modernised and a number of factories were built on the other side of the Dnieper. A telephone service was in operation by 1888, in time for the first of Kiev's annual contract fairs in 1889, which brought merchants to Kiev from all over Europe. In 1892 the first trains in Russia (the second in Europe) began to run from the city. As well as being the administrative and economic centre of the south-west part of the Russian Empire, Kiev was also the hub of the Ukrainian literary and national movement. By 1917 its population was half a million.

**The Revolutions

During the reign of Alexander III (1881–1894) Russia acquired lands in Central Asia. Nicholas II (1894–1917) was the last Russian tsar. In 1905 the first Russian revolution, which culminated in armed insurrections in both the cities and the countryside, and was particularly famous for its battles in Moscow, especially in the Presnya region, was severely suppressed; nevertheless it loosened the tsar's control over the country. It was of this that Vladimir Lenin wrote, 'It trained the ranks of the fighters who were victorious in 1917.' A constitution of a kind was granted. In 1914 after the beginning of the war with Germany the name of the capital was changed from the Germanic-sounding Petersburg to the Russian equivalent Petrograd ('grad' meaning city or town). In February 1917, in the third year of World War I, another revolution began in Russia. On 2 March Nicholas II abdicated and soon a provisional government was formed. It existed till October. On 25 October (7 November, new style) the Bolsheviks (Communists) led by Lenin seized power and the Soviet State was established.

By government decree on 16 November 1917, Moscow was re-established as the capital of the country, and the government moved to the Kremlin in March 1918. Nicholas and all his immediate family were executed in July 1918 at Ekaterinburg (now Sverdlovsk) in the Urals. Moscow has been the seat of the government ever since except for the winter of 1941–42 when the government moved to Kuibyshev because of the threat of German invasion.

The country was in a critical situation and the young Republic had to contend with the opposition of the White Russians (counter-revolutionaries) and with foreign intervention. Nationalist feelings and demands for the autonomy of the Ukraine had developed at the beginning of the 20th century, and during the civil war of 1918–1922 the Ukraine was one of the most fiercely contested areas. It was under both German and White Russian occupation, and had different nationalist governments. The Ukrainian Soviet Republic was first proclaimed in December 1917 and Kiev was the seat of several transitory Ukrainian governments although it was occupied by the Germans for a short while in 1918. In 1922 the Ukraine with Kharkov as its capital was one of the four original republics to form the USSR.

In 1924 Lenin died, Petrograd was renamed

Leningrad in his honour and Soviet leadership passed to Stalin.

Kiev resumed its position as capital and seat of Ukrainian government in 1934. In 1939 the western part of the Ukraine was added to the republic.

After the revolution the reconstruction of Moscow began on a grand scale. Now many of the old buildings, including half the churches, have been demolished and large new suburbs have been built. The first plan for the reconstruction of Moscow, drawn up in 1935, called for radical new building and alterations in the centre of the city. Gorky Street was widened and the Moskva Hotel and the Lenin Library built.

**Second World War

From 1941–1945 the Soviet Union joined the Allies to defeat the Axis powers. Leningrad was under siege by the Germans for almost 900 days. In August 1941 Nazi troops reached the outskirts of the city and it became part of the front line. Food supplies ran short, water and electricity were cut off, fuel stocks ran out, and public transport came to a standstill. About 650,000 people died in Leningrad during the blockade and more than 10,000 buildings were destroyed or damaged by bombs or artillery fire. Kiev too suffered dreadful damage and 195,000 Kievans died. Despite the drastic rebuilding necessary after the war, the three old divisions of the city still exist, and have retained their individuality. The German army came dangerously close to Moscow but was stopped on the outskirts in the winter of 1941–42; in 1965 Moscow, Leningrad and Kiev were all proclaimed Hero Cities, sharing the honour with Odessa, Sevastopol, Volgograd, Novorossiisk, Kerch and Brest Fortress. Moscow had not suffered much from the German air raids. Building work was held up by the war, but was later continued on an even grander scale. New avenues lined with vast buildings, such as Prospect Mira and Leninsky Prospect, were constructed and a few huge skyscrapers were built with a somewhat gothic appearance – the Ministry of Foreign Affairs and the new university are good examples.

1. The Arbat

2. Red Square and the Lenin Mausoleum

3. St Basil's Cathedral and the Spassky Tower

4. The Kremlin and Ivan the Great's Belfry

5. The gigantic Rossia Hotel and old churches nearby

6. Borodinsky Bridge across the Moskva river

7. **Statue of Alexander Pushkin in Gorky Street**

MOSCOW

We should like to suggest the following sightseeing plan:

Day 1 – *the Kremlin, city tour, Red Square, Bolshoi Theatre*
Day 2 – *Novodevichy Convent, a picture gallery, river boat, GUM and central market, circus*
Day 3 – *Folk Art Museum, a house-museum, a palace, Beryozka shop, puppet theatre*

However, Intourist will plan a full timetable for you, here as in Kiev. Our choice of highlights may not be theirs – or yours either, so we describe all the favourites.

Museum times are subject to change; it is best to check with Intourist to be sure, especially regarding closing days.

Day 1

The Kremlin

The cathedrals are open 10–6; closed Thurs. It is just as well to remember to keep to the proper places in the Kremlin so that you don't get whistled at.

Kremlin is a translation of the Russian word 'kreml' which means fortress. There are kremlins in a number of old Russians towns but none so well known as the Moscow Kremlin which serves as a synonym for the Soviet state and government.

**The Rivers
**The Gates

The Kremlin stands on an irregular triangle of ground covering 28 hectares (69 acres) above the river Moskva. From it an advancing enemy could be seen and a bell would be rung to call those within hearing to seek protection inside. It used to be surrounded by water: the river Moskva on the south, the Neglinnaya (now bricked in) on the south-west, and a deep moat which was dug in the early 16th century along the east wall. The main entrances to the Kremlin, the Spassky, Nikolsky, Trinity and Borovitsky Gates, were all protected by drawbridges on the far side of which were portcullises.

The first wooden walls around the Kremlin were built in the 12th century under Prince Yuri Dolgoruky, founder of Moscow. At that time it was a much smaller fortress at the confluence of the rivers Moskva and Neglinnaya. In the 14th century, during the reign of Prince Ivan Kalita, the Kremlin was considerably enlarged and the first two stone buildings were erected – the Cathedral of the Assumption (Uspensky Sobor) and the Cathedral of Archangel Michael (Arkhangelsky Sobor).

**The Walls

In 1367 the wooden fence was replaced by white limestone walls which protected the Kremlin from the fires which constantly ravaged Moscow, but these walls soon crumbled and were replaced at the end of the 15th century with the battlemented brick walls which stand today. The circumference of the walls is over 2 km (1 mile) and in some places they are as high as 19 m (62 ft). There are 20 towers, 5 of which are gates to the fortress. The towers were originally surmounted by battlements and each tower contained a firing platform. A platform for bowmen runs along the inside of the walls. The timber roofing which used to cover the platform was burnt down in the 18th century.

**The Towers

In the following description those towers which since 1937 have been decorated with illuminated red stars in place of the tsarist double-headed eagle are marked with an asterisk*. The main gate to the Kremlin is that opposite St. Basil's Cathedral on Red Square. It is known as the Spassky (Redeemer's) Gate* and was built in 1491 by Pietro Antonio Solario of Milan. It used to be entered by a drawbridge over the moat. In 1625 the Scottish architect Christopher Galloway added the Gothic tower and steeple, and a clock was installed. The present clock dates from 1851. The chime of the largest bell in the tower clock is broadcast on Moscow Radio, as is that of Big Ben on the BBC. Before the revolution there was an icon of the Redeemer above the gate, hence its name, and it was a strictly observed custom that everyone entering the Kremlin by this gate should bare his head and enter on foot.

The next large tower (moving in an anti-clockwise direction) is the Nikolsky Tower* near the Historical Museum. It was built in 1491 at the same time as the Spassky Tower, but was blown up in 1812 by Napoleon and rebuilt in 1820 by Bovet. It is named after the icon of St. Nicholas which used to hang over the gateway.

At the corner of the wall is the Sobakina Tower which was built particularly solidly, partly because it contained a secret well, important in time of siege, and also because it concealed a way out to the Neglinnaya which used to flow along the Kremlin wall. The Trinity Gate* was built in 1495 and is the tallest of all the Kremlin towers. It is approached by a bridge over the Alexandrovsky Gardens, constructed in place of the Neglinnaya, from the Kutafia Tower. This was one of the first stone bridges in Moscow and was built in 1516. The mounds beside the wall further along the garden are the remains of earthworks constructed by Peter the Great in 1707 when Charles XII of Sweden planned to attack Moscow.

The next large tower is the Borovitskaya (forest)* which was built in 1490, also by Solario, the upper half being added at the end of the 17th century. It was through its gate that Napoleon entered the Kremlin. At the corner nearest the Kamenny (stone) Bridge over the Moskva is the round Water-Hoist Tower*, so named in 1663 when craftsmen found a way to raise water from the river and convey it along an aqueduct to the Kremlin palaces and gardens. It was built in 1488 by Antonio Friasin, but was blown up in 1812 and rebuilt by Bovet in 1817. Along the river are five smaller towers. The first was used as a prison during the reign of Ivan the Terrible. The next is called the Tainitskaya Tower (Tower of Secrets) because of a secret underground passage which led from here down to the river. The gates were bricked up in 1930 but they can be seen from the road below.

The last corner tower is that of SS. Constantin and Helen˙ which was attached to a church of the same name. Next is Nabatnaya (alarm) Tower, from which a bell was rung in time of danger. The last tower is the Tsar's Tower which was added in 1860; Ivan the Terrible is said to have watched ceremonies in Red Square from a platform near the site of the present tower.

Inside the Kremlin, the central square is Cathedral

Square where the three principal cathedrals are situated.

**The Cathedrals

The Uspensky (Assumption) Cathedral on the north side of the square, is the largest. It was built in 1475–79 by the Italian architect Aristotle Fioravanti, who had spent many years in Russia studying the architecture of old Russian cities. The five-domed cathedral was built in the style of the 12th-century Uspensky Cathedral in Vladimir and it became Russia's principal church. The tsars were crowned here and the cathedral served as the burial vault of the Moscow metropolitans and patriarchs.

The walls of the cathedral are of white limestone and the drums beneath the domes and the vaulting are of brick. The exterior is divided into panels set off by columns and gables. On the west, south and north facades halfway up the walls is a belt of blind arcading.

The interior surprised visitors in the 15th century by its size and lightness. The walls are covered in frescoes dating from the 16th to 19th centuries. The five-tiered iconostasis, which was covered in chased silver gilt at the end of the 19th century, includes some fine icons of the 14th to 17th centuries. The icon of the Virgin of Vladimir is a copy of the 11th-century Byzantine icon which was in the cathedral but which is now in the Tretyakov Gallery. Originals still here, however, include the icon of St. George (early 12th-century Novgorodian school) and the icon of the Trinity (14th century).

Near the main entrance is the Tsar's Throne, which was carved in walnut in 1551 and which belonged to Ivan the Terrible. Known as the Throne of Monomakh, it is covered in carvings and inscriptions depicting Vladimir Monomakh's Thracian campaign. The shrine in the south-east corner contains the relics of Patriarch

Hermogen, killed by Polish invaders in 1612.

During the Napoleonic invasion the French soldiers turned the cathedral into a stable, using the icons as firewood. They took away with them 288 kilograms (5.25 cwt) of various gold articles and 5,000 kilograms (5 tons) of silver, much of which was lost during the subsequent retreat and which has not yet been recovered. The central chandelier, however, is made from silver captured from the French troops.

The Blagoveshchensky (Annunciation) Cathedral was designed as a chapel for Ivan III in early Moscow style in 1484–89. It was rebuilt in 1562–64 after a fire, with additions by builders from Pskov. The nine domes and the roof were covered in gilded copper and it became known as the 'Golden-domed'. In 1572 a new porch and steps were added which are called the Steps of Ivan the Terrible.

The floor of the cathedral is of polished tiles of agate jasper and the walls are covered in frescoes dating from the 16th century. The pillars bear portraits of Greek philosophers and of all the Moscow princes from Prince Daniel to Vasily III. The second and third tiers of the iconostasis include icons painted by Theophanes the Greek, Prokhor from Gorodets and Andrei Rublyov. Six of the icons in the third tier are attributed to Andrei Rublyov: 'The Transfiguration', 'The Entry into Jerusalem', 'The Purification of the Blessed Virgin', 'The Nativity', 'The Epiphany' and 'The Annunciation'. Other works of art which can be seen in the south gallery include the 13th-century 'Golden-Haired Christ', the 14th-century 'Cloaked Christ', and the 16th-century 'Our Lady of Vladimir'.

A narrow staircase in the north wall leads up to the choir where female members of the tsar's family used to sit during services.

The Arkhangelsky (Archangel Michael's) Cathedral was built on the site of a 14th-century church in

1505–09 by an Italian architect from Milan, Alevisio Novi, but it is in Russian style with only traces of Italian influence, particularly in the exterior. The north and south facades are divided into three sections, the east and west into five. Each section is made to stand out by pilasters and is surmounted by gables or fluted niches. The five domes are painted silver. The decorative white limestone portals on the north and west facades show Italian influence.

The interior walls are decorated with murals painted in 1652–66 by a large group of artists from several Russian towns. They depict scenes from every-day life and battle scenes as well as paintings of a religious and historical nature. On the south-west pillar is a portrait of Alexander Nevsky who defeated the Teutonic knights in 1242. The gilded carved wooden iconostasis contains icons dating mostly from the 15th to 17th centuries. That of the Archangel Michael is attributed to Andrei Rublyov.

From 1340 to 1700, first the smaller church which stood on the site and then the cathedral served as the burial vault of the grand princes of Moscow and the Russian tsars. There are portraits of many of the monarchs on the walls above the tombs. All the tsars from Ivan Kalita to Peter the Great, except for Boris Godunov whose body was exhumed in 1606, are buried here. The bronze encasements were added in 1903.

**The Bell-Tower

The Bell-Tower of Ivan the Great, which unites the various buildings of the Kremlin into a single architectural ensemble, is one of the most remarkable structures to be built in the 16th century. The lower part was built in 1532–43, and the belfry and cupola added in 1600 as famine relief work carried out under Boris Godunov. Below the cupola are three rows of Slavonic script which relate the circumstances under which the work was carried out.

The bell-tower is 81 m (266 ft) high, and when it was first built, it served as a watch-tower from which all Moscow and the vicinity within a radius of 30 km (19 miles) could be observed. There are 21 bells in the tower. In 1812 Napoleon, believing the cross on top of the dome to be pure gold, ordered it to be removed. However, it was found to be iron and those who had spread the rumour were shot.

**The Tsar Bell

At the foot of the Bell-Tower of Ivan the Great is the Tsar Kolokol (Tsar Bell), the largest bell in the world. It weighs over 200 tons and the fragment on the ground weighs 11.5 tons. It was cast in 1733–35 in a special casting pit inside the Kremlin by Ivan Motorin and his son Mikhail. After its completion the bell remained in the casting pit, but during the Kremlin fire of 1737 several cracks appeared and a large piece was broken off. The damage is thought to have been caused by the uneven cooling of the bell when cold water, used to extinguish the fire, fell on the bell. Almost a century later in 1836 the bell was raised from the casting pit and placed on its pedestal. The decorations include two inscriptions describing the history of its casting.

**Tsar Cannon

Not far from the Tsar Bell is the Tsar Cannon which has the largest calibre of any gun in the world. It was cast in 1586 at the Cannon Yard on the bank of the Neglinnaya where Teatralny Proyezd is today. It weighs 40 tons and is 5.3 m (17 ft) long with a calibre of 890 mm (35 in) and a barrel 15 cm (6 in) thick. It used to stand outside the Kremlin in Kitai-Gorod where it covered the approaches to Spassky Gate and the ford across the Moskva. A special carriage was required to fire it, but the present carriage was cast in 1835 for display purposes. It was probably called the Tsar Cannon on account of its size.

Behind the Blagoveshchensky (Annunciation) Cathedral is the Church of the Twelve Apostles and the Patriarch's Palace, built in 1656 for Patriarch Nikon on foundations of 1450. The four-storey palace includes part of the older residence of Boris Godunov. The church and palace now house a museum of 17th-century applied arts. The exhibits were taken from the reserve of the State Armoury Museum and include books, domestic utensils, household linen and clothing. The 17th-century carved wooden iconostasis in the church was formerly in the Kremlin Monastery of the Ascension, demolished in the 1930s.

The Church of the Deposition of the Robe (Tserkov Rizpolozheniya) is a small, single-domed church standing between the Cathedral of the Assumption (Uspensky Sobor) and the Palace of Facets. It was built in 1484–86 by masons from Pskov on the site of an older church of the same name. This church served as a private chapel for the patriarch before the Church of the Twelve Apostles was built. The interior is decorated with frescoes painted by court painters who had also helped to paint those in the Cathedral of the Assumption.

Behind the Church of the Deposition of the Robe one can see the eleven gilded domes of the Upper Saviour's Church (Verkhospasskaya Tserkov), built in 1635–36 over the Tsarina's Golden Room in the Terem Palace. The church was used by the royal family. This church is very picturesque amongst the other more austere churches and cathedrals. The cupolas have long red brick drums which are decorated with blue and green tiles. The copper roof is 18th century work.

**Palace of Facets

The Granovitaya Palata (Palace of Facets) on the west side of Cathedral Square is the oldest public building in Moscow. Its name derives from the shape of the stone facings on the side looking onto Cathedral Square. It was built in 1473–91 by the Italian architects Marco Ruffo and Pietro Antonio. The ground floor rooms were designed for administrative purposes and the upper floor as a single chamber for receptions. The chamber, 500 sq. m (5380 sq ft) in area, has four cross vaults supported by one central pillar. The present murals were painted in the 1880s by the Belousovs from the town of Palekh after designs of 1683. The iron ribs of the vaulting are gilded and carry inscriptions in Slavonic lettering. Above the carved portal is a look-out room from which the tsarinas and their daughters watched the receptions as custom forbade any women to be present.

**Grand Kremlin Palace

The Grand Kremlin Palace was built in 1838–49 by a team of architects under the supervision of Konstantin Thon on the site of an earlier palace. It was the residence of the imperial family during their visits to Moscow. It is now a government building where the Supreme Soviets of the U.S.S.R. and of the Russian Federation meet, and where official receptions are held.

**St. George's Hall

The grandest of the old halls is St. George's Hall, named after the tsarist military order of St. George. Along the walls are marble plaques inscribed in gold with the names of officers and military units decorated with the Cross of St. George, the highest award in tsarist Russia.

Doors in the centre of St. George's Hall lead into the

Hall of St. Vladimir, and from here one can go into the Terem Palace built in 1635. These are the old private chambers of the tsar on the site of still older chambers built for Vasily II and Ivan the Terrible.

**The Armoury

The Oruzheinaya Palata (Armoury), where the tsar's regalia and ambassadorial gifts are kept, is the oldest of all Russian museums. It is usually open for group excursions only and tickets are best obtained through Intourist.

The museum exhibits are treasures of the tsars which were collected through the centuries. In the reign of Ivan III (1462–1505) there were already so many treasures that they had to be housed in a special building called the Treasure Court which was built for this purpose between the Annunciation and Archangel Cathedrals. Weapons and armour were also made in the same building, which gave the collection and the present building its name. Most of the treasures were made in the Kremlin workshops. The collection grew particularly large under Ivan the Terrible and, when Moscow was threatened by the Crimean Tatars, 450 sledges were needed to move the treasure to Novgorod. During the 16th and 17th centuries the treasure was augmented by gifts from foreign monarchs and ambassadors. In the reign of Peter the Great the Kremlin craftsmen were moved to the new capital of St. Petersburg and work in the Kremlin workshops almost came to a halt. At the beginning of the 19th century the treasures were moved into the Imperial Palace Museum opposite the Arsenal and Senate buildings and in 1851 into the present building.

**Hall I – Weapons and Armour

Weaponry, war trophies and gifts, 13th to 18th centuries. Among the collection of helmets on Stand 1 note the small one of little Prince Ivan, son of Ivan the Terrible; an inscription says that it was made for the prince, who was then four years old, by order of his father in 1557.

On Stand 3 is the helmet of Tsar Mikhail Romanov, which has a finely polished surface inlaid with gilt and decorated with diamonds, rubies and emeralds. Among the sabres are lavishly decorated gold and silver ones studded with precious stones which were worn by the tsars on ceremonial occasions. Also here are the sabres of Minin and Pozharsky who headed the army which drove the Poles out of Moscow in 1612. They were made in Egypt and Persia respectively.

Stand 5 displays Russian arms of the reign of Peter the Great and trophies from the Northern War (1700–21). In the centre is a bas-relief of Peter the Great beaten in pewter. Among the Swedish trophies from the war are a silver mace bearing the crest of Gustavus Adolphus Vasa and a bible published in Stockholm in 1703 bearing the monogram of Charles XII.

Stand 6 has a display of 16th-century pistols and European armour of the 15th to 17th centuries. In the centre is a suit of equestrian armour cast by Kunz Lochner and presented to Tsar Feodor in 1584 as a gift from King Stefan Batory of Poland. To the right of the stand are three which were made for the royal children in the 17th century. These were only worn on ceremonial occasions.

**Hall II – Russian Gold and Silver

Religious and secular items, 12th to 17th centuries. One of the earliest pieces of silver on display is a 12th-century chalice given to the Cathedral of the Saviour in Transfiguration in Pereslavl-Zalessky by Prince Yuri Dolgoruky, founder of Moscow. The fine work of Kiev craftsmen is shown here on the Ryazan

Treasure which dates from the 12th or 13th century, discovered in Old Ryazan in 1822. The treasure includes two heavy necklets decorated with coloured enamel and filigree, a bracelet, rings, ear-rings, and images of the saints. Novgorodian work is represented by a 14th-century jasper chalice in a silver filigree case studded with precious stones, and 14th-century dippers in the shape of a sauceboat. Also on display are gold and silver dippers which were used for drinking mead. These here were made by Moscow craftsmen in the 16th century, and include one smelted out of a single nugget which belonged to Boris Godunov. The highly decorated gospel was given to the Cathedral of the Assumption in 1571 by Ivan the Terrible. The gold cover is picked out with enamel and precious stones with pictures of Christ and the saints linked by inscriptions in blackened gold. There is a large collection of drinking vessels on display. The items dating from the second half of the 17th century are particularly lavish with bright enamelwork studded with jewels. Among these is a gold cup belonging to Tsar Alexei Mikhailovich which is covered in green enamel painted with bright flowers, the gold mounting for the icon of the Virgin of Vladimir studded with precious stones, including two emeralds weighing 100 carats each, and two gold-covered gospels with emerald-and-ruby-studded enamel.

Also on display in this hall are boxes, knives, forks, cups, and caskets, and a collection of Russian and foreign clocks and watches of the 16th to 18th centuries. The gilded copper watch in the form of a book belonged to Ivan the Terrible and the wooden watch was made in the 19th century by Russian craftsmen.

**Hall III – Silver and Jewellery

Baroque, rococo and Fabergé, 18th to 20th centuries. At the beginning of the 18th century St. Petersburg, the new capital, became the centre of the

Russian silver and gold trades. In the middle of the 18th century the predominant style was Russian baroque and rococo with very lavish ornamentation and bright enamel. On display is a collection of snuff-boxes made of gold, silver, mother-of-pearl, tortoise-shell, ivory and porcelain. Many of them are decorated with precious stones and enamel portraits. The flat snuff-box bearing an enamel portrait of Peter the Great was made in 1717 by Andrei Osov, one of the first Russian miniaturists. A large, round, gold snuff-box has a plated bas-relief portrait of the Empress Elizabeth. Further on is a collection of silver dating from 1770 to 1825, the period of Russian classicism, much plainer in decoration. In the centre of the stand is an oval gold dish presented to Catherine II by Prince Potyomkin. A little further on are two small crowns woven out of silver laurel leaves which are said to have been used during the ceremony of Pushkin's marriage to Natalia Goncharova in 1831.

The last section in this hall shows examples of the work of the famous jewellers' firms which grew up in Moscow and St. Petersburg after 1830. The work of Fabergé is well represented. One of the most fascinating examples is a silver Easter egg, on the outside of which is engraved a map of the Trans-Siberian Railway. Inside is a gold clock-work model of a Trans-Siberian express with a platinum engine with a ruby headlamp. The carriages are inscribed with the usual inscriptions, such as 'Smokers', 'Ladies Only' and 'Clerics', and have windows made of crystal. Another egg contains a gold model of the royal yacht, Standard. The yacht is set in a sea of rock crystal and the crystal egg has two pear-shaped pearl pendants. Another astonishing exhibit is a vase of rock-crystal with a pansy decoration. If a button on the flower stem is pressed, the petals open revealing miniature portraits of the children of Nicholas II in frames of small diamonds.

** Hall IV – Vestments

This hall contains vestments of silk, velvet and brocade, woven and embroidered with gold and encrusted with jewels and pearls. They belonged to the imperial family, patriarchs and metropolitan bishops.

** Hall V – Foreign Gold and Silver

Mainly foreign gifts, 13th to 19th centuries. Most of the items on display in this hall were gifts to the tsars from ambassadors on behalf of their country. The first exhibits are of Dutch silver made in Amsterdam in the 16th century, many decorated with the Dutch tulip motif.

The next section is a collection of English silver, mostly made in London in the 16th and 17th centuries. In 1553 Richard Chancellor was received in Moscow by Ivan the Terrible and was the first of a long succession of ambassadors to the Russian Court. The earliest item is a flat goblet, made in 1557, and thought to have been presented to Ivan the Terrible by an English merchant.

Silver from Poland and Sweden is in the next section. Many of the gifts from Poland in the 17th century were made in Danzig, but a number of the items here were made in Germany where they were bought by Polish tradesmen. The collection from Sweden is the largest of all and comprises about 200 items, all made in the 17th century. Some of these were made in Augsberg, including the two oval basins which were a gift from Queen Christina to Tsar Alexei. The two globes, depicting the earthly and heavenly spheres supported by the figures of Neptune and Atlas, were also made by German craftsmen and were brought to Moscow as gifts from Charles X. The work of Swedish silversmiths is represented by a number of pieces including candlesticks, flasks, tumblers, filigree cups and a water bowl in the shape of a silver swan.

The next stand is a display of gifts from Denmark, also mostly made by German craftsmen.

Further on are silver and gold vessels made in Nuremburg in the 15th to 17th centuries. There is a large collection of drinking-cups and goblets in various shapes, some in the form of a fruit or an animal.

At the end of the hall are some foreign dinner and tea services. The large silver service is only part of one consisting of over 3,000 pieces given by Catherine II in 1772 to Prince Orlov. It was ordered from Rottiers et Fils, but the order was so large that they were obliged to subcontract part of it. The Sèvres tea, coffee and dessert services were presented to Alexander I by Napoleon when the Treaty of Tilsit was signed.

**Hall VI – Regalia

Garments and regalia of the royal family. At the beginning of the hall on the left are the thrones of the tsars. Ivan the Terrible's was made in Western Europe and is decorated with ivory carvings. The second throne, covered with thin plates of gold and studded with 2,200 precious stones and pearls, was given to Boris Godunov by Shah Abbas of Persia. The third was made in Moscow for Mikhail Romanov from a throne of Iranian origin belonging to Ivan the Terrible. The next throne was presented to Tsar Alexei Romanov by a group of Armenian merchants. Made in Persia, it is decorated with 1,223 precious stones and 876 diamonds which have given it the name of the 'Diamond Throne'. The last throne is that used in the first years of the reign of Peter the Great when he shared power with his elder brother, Ivan, and his sister Sophia was regent. The two seats in front were used by the two tsars and the hidden seat behind by Sophia who used to prompt the boys with the right answers to ambassadors' questions.

The earliest crown on display is the 'Cap of

Monomakh' which was made by oriental craftsmen in the 13th or 14th centuries and is thought to have been given to the Grand Prince Vladimir Monomakh of Kiev by the Emperor of Byzantium. It is made of finely wrought gold lace smelted onto a strip of gold lead, surmounted by a pearl-tipped gold cross and edged with a band of sable.

The Kazan Cap was made in Moscow for Ivan the Terrible to commemorate the capture of Kazan. Also exhibited is the regalia made in Moscow for the coronation of Tsar Mikhail Romanov, the regalia brought to Moscow from Greece for Tsar Alexei Romanov, and the diamond coronets made in Moscow between 1682 and 1689 for Peter the Great and his brother Ivan. There are only two crowns of imperial Russia in the armoury, that of Anna Ivanovna, encrusted with numerous diamonds and a large ruby, and the crown of Catherine I.

The last section of this hall contains Russian costumes from the 16th century. Until the end of the 17th century the most usual garment was a long loose caftan; these include one belonging to Peter the Great. From the end of the 17th century shorter, closer-fitting clothes were worn with short breeches reaching just below the knee.

Beyond the men's garments is a display of accessories and jewellery. Ear-rings were worn by men in Russia until the reign of Peter the Great. At the end of the hall are a number of dresses, including coronation dresses, which belonged to the empresses and tsars' wives.

**Halls VII and VIII – Harnesses

The harnesses in these two halls are extremely exotic. Most of them were made in Russia but some were gifts to the Russian court from foreign countries, in particular from Poland which regularly sent saddles to the tsar.

The display begins with a collection of 16th and 17th-century German, Polish and English harnesses. The oldest saddles here were gifts to Boris Godunov from the King of Poland. The German saddles were made in the second half of the 17th century and are decorated with embroidery.

Further on are a number of Persian harnesses, mostly gifts from the Shah of Persia. A particularly exotic saddle is that in a gold frame, covered in velvet and embroidered with gold thread and decorated with rubies, emeralds and turquoise.

The earliest Russian saddle on display was made during the reign of Ivan the Terrible. It is covered with velvet, embroidered with golden double-headed eagles. There are a number of childrens' saddles, no less ornate than those for adults, including one made in 1642 for the Tsarevich Alexei Mikhailovich.

**Hall IX – Carriages

The oldest carriage is a 16th-century English one thought to have been a gift to Boris Godunov from Elizabeth I. The child's coach and closed sledge were made at the end of the 17th century for Peter the Great when he was a child.

An unusual carriage is that in which Empress Elizabeth travelled from St. Petersburg to Moscow for her coronation. It was drawn by 23 horses – one pair and seven threes. The most lavish of all, however, is the French carriage made in Paris in 1757. This one, with carved gilt wood made to represent sea foam and breaking waves, has panels painted by Francois Bouchet. It was presented to Empress Elizabeth by Count Razumovsky.

The newest section of the museum houses gifts made to the Soviet Union by foreign countries.

Palace of Congresses and other buildings

The Palace of Congresses was completed in 1961 for the 22nd Soviet Communist Party Congress. It was built deep down into the ground, the height of a 5-storey house, so that it would not be taller than the rest of the Kremlin ensemble. The presidium seats and the rostrum can be lowered to form an orchestra pit as the building is also used for concerts, ballet and opera.

The Arsenal is the long, yellow building forming a quadrangle between the Trinity and Nikolsky Towers. Peter the Great planned it as a storehouse for arms and ammunition, but it suffered repeatedly from fires. The present building was completed in 1828. Plans were made in the 19th century to open a museum of the 1812 war in the building. 875 cannon captured from the French army were placed along the south-east wall where they remain today, but the museum never materialised.

The building of the Council of Ministers faces the south-eastern facade of the Arsenal. Before the revolution it was the Senate building. The domed roof belongs to a large circular hall, once known as the White Hall or the Catherine Hall and now used for plenary meetings of the Central Committee of the Communist Party.

A Tour of the City

A city tour is very useful to enable you to get your bearings and a better idea of the lie of the land.

Moscow is by far the largest city in the Soviet Union. Originally a small defence post on the Moskva river, from which it takes its name, Moscow owes its importance largely to its geographical position. Today it is the main junction of all the road and rail arteries. Building is continuing at an astounding rate, both in the suburbs and in the centre, where it is planned that new wide roads will converge.

**Street Plan of Moscow

The city has developed outwards from the Kremlin in concentric circles which have been formed on the line of the old fortifications. The Bulvarnoye Koltso (boulevard ring) and Sadovoye Koltso (garden ring) serve as easily recognisable landmarks. The Bulvarnoye Koltso, which has a line of trees and gardens down the middle, is the nearest to the centre and forms a semi-circle on the northern banks of the river Moskva. The Sadovoye Koltso is a very wide, busy street which intercepts all the main streets radiating from the centre.

The boundary of Moscow is marked by the circular bypass which lies at an average distance of 25 km (16 miles) from the city centre. There are a number of satellite townships outside which count as regions of the city proper, but the ring is still a useful guide for orientation. Within the ring a number of new roads are being built to follow the concentric circle plan.

**Lenin Hills

A good vantage point with a panoramic view over the city is Lenin Hills, in front of the main building of Moscow University. The University was founded in 1755 by Russia's great scientist and encyclopaedist, Mikhail Lomonosov, and is named after him. It is the largest university in the country and has over 22,000 students attending its 14 faculties.

**Moscow University

It is housed in a number of buildings in the city centre and also since 1953 in the sky-scraper on Lenin Hills. The main buildings in the centre are the two opposite the Alexandrovsky Gardens on either side of Herzen

Street. The oldest building, on the right as one faces Herzen Street, was built by Matvei Kazakov in 1786–93. It was badly damaged in the 1812 fire, after which it was restored and altered by Gigliardi, who was responsible for the facade with the 8-column colonnade and the semi-circular assembly hall with Ionic columns and murals. The monuments to Alexander Herzen and Nikolai Ogaryov by Nikolai Andreyev in front of the building were erected in 1922.

The building on the other side of Herzen Street, still known as the 'new' building, was built by Tyurin in 1836 in classical style. Behind it is the Church of the Apparition (Znamenskaya Tserkov) which was built at the end of the 17th century in Russian baroque style. The monument to Mikhail Lomonosov in front of the university was made by Kozlovsky and erected in 1857.

**New University Building

The new building on Lenin Hills was designed by Rudnyev and built in 1949–53. It is used chiefly by the scientific departments of the university and for accommodation. The main building is 240 m (787 ft) high, including the spire, and the main facade is 450 m (492 yd) long. The whole university complex here, which is situated on a site of 166 hectares (415 acres), comprises 27 blocks and 10 ancillary buildings. To inspect all the premises one would have to walk 150 km (93 miles).

**Red Square

Red Square (Krasnaya Ploshchad) is the main square of the city where demonstrations and military parades take place. Its name dates from the 17th century, the word 'krasnaya' meaning 'beautiful' in Old Russian. The square is 695 m (760 yds) long and 130 m (142 yds) wide. The best view of the square is to be obtained from the windows of the Historical Museum which is on the northern side. To the south stands St. Basil's Cathedral with the Minin and Pozharsky Monument in front, to the west the Kremlin wall and the Lenin Mausoleum, and to the east GUM, pronounced 'goom', the State Department Store.

**St. Basil's Cathedral

The Cathedral of the Intercession (Pokrovsky Sobor) or St. Basil's as it is more usually called, was built in 1555–60 by order of Ivan the Terrible to commemorate the conquest of the Tatar City of Kazan on the Volga. Ivan the Terrible's first plan was for eight churches to be built on Red Square, each church being dedicated to the saints on whose days he won his battles. One stone and seven wooden churches were built in 1552, but Ivan the Terrible was dissatisfied and ordered them to be demolished. The task of building new churches was given to Barma and Postnik, two architects whom recent historical evidence has shown were probably one and the same person, Postnik Yakovlev, whose nickname was Barma. A new plan was drawn up, this time for one large cathedral surrounded by seven subsidiary churches. However, seven small churches would have spoilt the symmetry of the design so the architect(s) built eight.

The central cathedral, was named Pokrovsky Sobor (Cathedral of the Intercession) because the chief victory in the campaign fell on the day of the Intercession. The more popular name of St. Basil's was taken from a church built close to the cathedral in 1588 which was dedicated to the memory of a holy man named Vasili (Basil), a Muscovite who exercised a certain amount of influence over Ivan the Terrible.

There is a legend that when the cathedral was completed Ivan ordered the eyes of the architect(s) to be put out so that he (or they) could not build a similar cathedral elsewhere. It is known that when first completed the cathedral was painted in more subdued colours and that it was only in the 18th century that it was painted as it is now with the detail picked out in different colours. The exotic grandeur of the cathedral makes it one of the best and most striking examples of old Russian architecture.

Among the more interesting sights inside the cathedral are the iconostasis of the Trinity Church, the 'Entry into Jerusalem' icon in the same church and the interior decoration of the Church of St. Alexander of Svir.

**Lobnoye Mesto

Close to St. Basil's Cathedral is Lobnoye Mesto, a round platform of white stone constructed early in the 16th century. The Russian name for this platform, which is derived from the word 'forehead', has come to mean 'execution place'. Executions were not carried out on the platform, however, but near it. The first historical mention of Lobnoye Mesto is when Ivan the Terrible used it to make a public confession of misdeeds to the assembled people. At that time it was a round brick structure with a roof supported by pillars and surrounded by a wooden fence. In 1786 it was faced with rough stone and the roof was removed. Until the reign of Peter the Great all edicts and decrees were read aloud here. The tsar used to present himself to his people here once a year and he also presented the heir-apparent when the latter reached the age of 16. All religious processions stopped by the Lobnoye Mesto while the chief clergyman present blessed the people from the platform.

**Minin and Pozharsky Statue

The statue of Minin and Pozharsky by Ivan Martos in front of St. Basil's Cathedral originally stood in the middle of Red Square. The turn of the 17th century is known as the time of troubles in Russian history. A variety of claimants to the throne appeared, and most were supported by the Poles. At one point Polish troops were threateningly near to the Kremlin but they were driven from the country in 1612 by an army of volunteers led by a meat merchant, Kosma Minin, and Prince Pozharsky. The statue of these two heroes was erected in 1818 from money collected by public donation. The two bas-relief ornaments on the pedestal of the monument depict episodes from the war.

**Lenin Mausoleum

The Lenin Mausoleum stands by the Kremlin wall. It is open 10–1; Sun. 10–2 (in winter 10–3); closed Mon. and Fri. To avoid standing in the long queue, tourists should ask Intourist to arrange a special time for an accompanied visit.

The body of Vladimir Lenin (1870–1924), the founder of the Communist Party and the Soviet State, whose real name was Ulyanov, lies here. Stalin's body also lay in the mausoleum from his death in 1953 until 1961, when it was removed by popular demand and buried near the Kremlin wall among other Communist leaders, including Frunze, Kirov, Sverdlov, Dzerzhinsky, Brezhnev, Andropov and Chernenko.

The building of the mausoleum was constructed in 1930 by Shchusev and is generally agreed to be well designed, harmonising with the older structures surrounding the square. It is made of red granite with black and grey labradorite. The present building replaced a wooden mausoleum which was erected after Lenin's death in 1924.

Steps lead up on both sides of the mausoleum to the roof where members of the government stand to watch parades and demonstrations in the square.

Two guards stand at the entrance to the mausoleum.

Steps lead down to the underground vault where the embalmed body lies in a glass sarcophagus. A railing surrounds the sacophagous and four guards stand nearby.

**Historical Museum

The Historical Museum stands on the north side of Red Square. It is open 10–6; Wed. 11–7; Fri. 12–7; closed Tuesday and the first Monday of each month. The building was constructed in 1874–83 by the architect Sherwood and the engineer Semyonov under the influence of 17th-century Russian architecture. The museum was initiated by Moscow University and the first 11 halls were open in 1883. It now has 300,000 exhibits and is the biggest repository of historical material and documents tracing the origin and history of the peoples of the Soviet Union from ancient times until the 1917 Revolution.

The first seven halls carry the story up to the 1st century A.D. The painting 'Stone Age' on the ceiling of the second hall is the work of the artist Vasnetsov and was commissioned for this hall in 1883–85.

Hall 9 contains archaeological finds from Novgorod dating from the 9th to 15th centuries. There are models of old Novgorodian churches as well as a collection of 14th and 15th century icons from Novgorod and Pskov.

Hall 13 contains a number of interesting exhibits showing the development of central Russia in the 14th and 15th centuries. Icons include the icon of 'The Virgin Mary with Sergei Radonezh', attributed to the school of Andrei Rublyov. There are fragments of the wooden streets of Novgorod which are thought to have been relaid 32 times in the course of 700 years, and part of the bows of a rowing boat dating from the 12th century. The fresco is a contemporary reconstruction of the Moscow Kremlin during the 16th century.

Hall 15 contains a number of beautifully illustrated manuscripts and the first book to be published in Russia, the Apostles of 1564.

Hall 20 relates the history of the beginning of the 18th century when St. Petersburg was founded by Peter the Great. There are many documents connected with the reforms carried out by Peter and garments belonging to the tsar.

Hall 23 relates the history of the second half of the 18th century, in particular the Peasants' Revolt of 1773–74. Above a portrait of Catherine II (1762–96) is one of the peasant leader Pugachev painted by an unknown artist in 1774. The iron cage in which Pugachev was brought to Moscow after the revolt had been suppressed is also displayed.

Hall 28, the walls of which are covered with banners captured from the French army and of the Russian regiments, contains exhibits pertaining to the 1812 war. On the right of the hall is a marble bust of Napoleon by an unknown artist which was brought to Russia in order to be erected in the main square of Moscow. The field kitchen and sledge which Napoleon used during the campaign is also here.

The remaining halls illustrate the history of the 19th century, including the Crimean War and the abolition of serfdom.

Halls 38 and 39 are devoted to scientific, literary, and artistic developments.

The last hall, 40, contains documents relating to the 1917 Revolution and the personal belongings and arms of the revolutionaries who stormed the Winter Palace in St. Petersburg.

**GUM

GUM (pronounced goom) Department Store – Red Square. Open Mon. Sat. 8 a.m.–9 p.m. GUM was built in 1888–94 by Pomerantsev in pseudo-Russian style as commercial arcades for nearly 1,000 small shops. It is now the country's largest shop. There is a souvenir department by the fountain in the middle of the central aisle, and the record department is also on the ground floor.

**Bolshoi Theatre

Sverdlov Square. This theatre was formerly known as the Great Imperial Theatre. It was built by Bovet in 1824 and restored by Cavos after a fire in 1854. The statue above the Ionic portico is of Phoebus in the Sun Chariot. The ballet company is known all over the world for its incomparable dancing. Russian and foreign operas are performed to enthusiastic, knowledgeable audiences. The orchestra is one of the best in the country.

Day 2

Novodevichy Convent, a picture gallery, a ride on a river boat, on the Metro (the underground), the central market, the circus.

**Novodevichy Convent

Novodevichy Monastyr (convent) – Bolshaya Pirogovskaya Street 2 (near the Sportivnaya metro station). Open 1 March – 30 Sept. 11–6; 1 Oct. – 28 Feb. 10.30–4.30; closed Tuesday and first Monday of each month.

Novodevichy Convent is one of the most interesting historical and architectural monuments in Moscow. It was founded in 1524 by Grand Prince Vasili Ioanovich to commemorate the union of Smolensk and Moscow. It formed a stronghold on the road to Smolensk and Lithuania and was enclosed by fortified walls with twelve towers.

Novodevichy was a convent for ladies of noble birth

and many historical figures ended their lives here. When Tsar Feodor died in 1598, his widow, Irina, and her brother, Boris Godunov, came to the convent. Tsar Feodor had been almost imbecile for a number of years before his death and power had been in the hands of his brother-in-law, Boris, but he realised that if he assumed power immediately he would be faced with opposition. His calculations proved right as he was soon entreated by the Patriarch and a number of nobles to leave the convent.

Peter the Great's elder sister, Princess Sophia, was banished to the convent in 1679 by her brother. In 1698 the Streltsy, whom she had supported in their revolt against the tsar, were hanged along the walls of the convent with their hands clasped in a begging attitude. Sophia, who had become Sister Susanna in the convent, had her hair shorn and was banished to a tower where she died in 1704. Her sisters, Yekaterina, Maria, and Fedosia, also lived in the convent.

Peter the Great, unlike other Russian tsars, saw little good in monasteries and convents. At one time he turned the Novodevichy Convent into a home for abandoned babies and he later issued an order that war veterans should be offered shelter in the convent.

Napoleon visited the monastery in 1812, but left it untouched until the last day of the French occupation when he ordered that it should be blown up. Barrels of gunpowder were set up in the convent, but a nun named Sara succeeded in extinguishing the fuses just in time and the convent remained undamaged.

The Preobrazhenskaya Tserkov (Church of the Transfiguration) is the first church the visitor sees when entering the convent through the main entrance. It was built in 1687–88 in Moscow baroque style over the gateway. The seven-tier iconostasis which was painted in 1687 by Kremlin craftsmen is of particular interest.

Nearby are the Lopukhinskiye Palaty (Lopukhin Chambers), a two-storey building erected in 1687–8 for the daughter of Tsar Alexei and sister of Peter the Great, Tsarevna Yekaterina. The first wife of Peter the Great, Evdokia Lopukhin, lived here from 1727 to 1731 and the building has been called after her ever since.

Smolensky Sobor (Smolensk Cathedral) was the main church of the convent. It was dedicated to Our Lady of Smolensk, which was an icon of the Virgin Mary brought to Kiev from Greece by the Greek Tsarevna Anna and thence to the cathedral in Smolensk. In 1398 the icon was moved to the Cathedral of the Annunciation in the Kremlin and now it is in the Tretyakov Gallery.

The cathedral was built in 1524–5 by the architect Aleviz Fryazin. The side aisles and galleries were added at the end of the 17th century. The brick walls of the cathedral are set off by the architectural details in white stone. Of the three arched entrances with carved cornices, also of white stone, those on the west and north facades remain in their original form.

The interior of the cathedral is covered in 16th century murals. The carved wooden iconostasis is worthy of special attention; it has 84 intricately carved columns and was the work of about 50 craftsmen under Konstantin Mikhailov in 1685. The icons date from the 16th and 17th centuries and were painted by the best Muscovite masters. The icon of Christ on the right-hand side of the first tier of the iconostasis and the icons on the doors of the sanctuary were painted by the famous 17th-century artist, Simeon Ushakov.

In the centre of the cathedral stands a large chalice which was made in 1685 and is decorated with brightly painted and embossed tulips and roses.

In the cathedral are the tombs of Princess Sophia, the first wife of Peter the Great, Evdokia Lopukhin, Tsarevna Anna, and the daughter of Ivan the Terrible.

The cathedral now houses a museum of Russian applied arts of the 16th and 17th centuries. The exhibits include embroidery, paintings, fabrics, woodwork, and metalwork. Along the south wall are exhibited the private possessions of Princess Sophia. There is also a large collection of 16th and 17th century books, beautifully illuminated and illustrated, bound in leather and decorated with gold, silver, and jewels.

The belfry is situated near the east wall of the convent. This is contrary to Russian custom, in which belfries were always built on the western side of the main buildings, but the site was chosen as it was thought that the belfry would be more striking on this side of the convent. It is indeed a fine example of the best architecture of the time and is considered by many to be superior to the Bell-Tower of Ivan the Great in the Kremlin. The belfry was completed in 1690, is 72 m (236 ft) in height and consists of six octagonal tiers of varying width and height. Around the base of each tier is an open-arched gallery. The belfry, which was built of brick, is decorated with limestone details which give it an air of lightness in spite of its size.

Uspenskaya Tserkov (Church of the Assumption) was built in 1687, but was badly damaged in a fire in 1796 after which it was rebuilt and much altered. In place of the five cupolas only one was rebuilt. It is now open for religious services with particularly large crowds on feast days.

Trapeznaya Palata (Refectory). The refectory was built at the same time as the Church of the Assumption which adjoins it. It is a large hall with no supporting pillars which was the refectory for nuns and the hall where guests were entertained on feast days. After the fire of 1796 the refectory was rebuilt, but without the open galleries which formerly ran along the western facade of the building.

Near the refectory is the Palata Iriny Godunovoy

(The Chamber of Irina Godunov), sister of Boris Godunov, who came to live in the convent after the death of her husband, Tsar Feodor, in 1598. The building was completed in the same year and was then surmounted by a wooden chamber with a lavishly painted roof. The building was considerably altered at the end of the 18th century.

To the south of the convent, but still within the walls, is a cemetery with many famous graves. The writers Gogol and Chekhov are buried here, and also Stalin's wife Nadezhda Alliluyeva. Prominent statesmen (Khrushchev among them), artists and military officers are still buried here in the new part of the cemetery.

The visit to a picture gallery could be to see Russian art at the Tretyakov, world art at the Pushkin or icons at the Rublyov Museum.

**Tretyakov Gallery

Lavrushinsky Pereulok 10. Check with Intourist as the Gallery has been closed for restoration.

The Tretyakov Gallery consists exclusively of Russian art from early religious works of the 10th century until the present day.

The foundation of this collection was laid by the art collectors Pavel and Sergei Tretyakov. Pavel Tretyakov began his collection with a number of lithographs and engravings and only later turned to paintings, in particular contemporary Russian art, and then to icons. His brother Sergei collected West European paintings and Russian sculpture. When Sergei died in 1892, he bequeathed his whole collection to Pavel, who in the same year gave the whole collection, then comprising 3,500 works of art, to the city of Moscow.

After the Revolution the works of West European artists were transferred to the Pushkin Museum of

Fine Arts. Since then the collection has grown and, although a new wing was built to accommodate works of the Soviet period, the present building, designed by Vasnetsov in 1898 to house the collection, is far too small. (A new gallery on the Krymsky Embankment opposite the main entrance to Gorky Park now houses recent acquisitions.)

In the forecourt is a copy of Yevgeny Vuchetich's sculpture 'Swords into Ploughshares', presented to the United Nations by the Soviet Union.

**Pushkin Gallery

Pushkin Fine Arts Museum – Volkhonka Street 12, near Kropotkinskaya metro station. Open 10–8 (Sun 10–6); closed Mon. The museum, first known as Alexander II's museum, opened in 1812. The building was designed by Academician Klein and completed in the same year.

After the Hermitage in Leningrad this is the largest museum in the country. It was first planned, however, not as a museum of original works of art, but as an educational museum serving the needs of Moscow University. For this purpose, many copies of Egyptian, Greek and Roman works of art were made under the direction of Professor Tsvetayev, the first director of the museum.

The museum collection was greatly enhanced by a number of donations, most notably those by the collector Golenishchev of Ancient Egyptian Art and Ancient Coptic Art. In 1925 the collection of West European paintings which had belonged to Sergei Tretyakov was moved here from the Tretyakov Gallery, and also the renowned collection of French art which had belonged before the Revolution to two patrons of art, Morozov and Shchukin.

In the first hall of the gallery is the collection of

Ancient Egyptian Art dating from the 4th century B.C. to the 1st century A.D.

Hall 2 contains works of art dating from the 3rd century B.C. to the 7th century A.D. from Babylon, Assyria, Persia, etc.

Spanish and Italian art (Halls 28 and 29) is represented by such arists as Murillo, Jose de Ribera, Botticelli, Romano, and Fetti.

Hall 30 is devoted to Dutch art of the 17th century, including works by Ruisdael, Rembrandt, Steen, and Ostade. The next hall contains works by Flemish artists including Rubens and Van Dyck.

One of the most treasured sections is the collection of French paintings in Halls 27 to 22. Artists included here are Poussin (Hall 27), Watteau and David (Hall 25), Delacroix, Rousseau, and Gericault (Hall 24), Cezanne, Courbet, Manet, Matisse, Gauguin, Van Gogh, Picasso and Monet (Halls 23 and 22).

**Rublyov (Rublev) Museum

Andrei Rublyov Museum of Ancient Art – Pryamikov Square 10. Open 11–6; Mon. and Tues. 1–8; Sun. 11–6; closed Wed. The museum is inside the walls of the former Spaso-Andronikov Monastery which was founded in 1360 by Bishop Alexei of Moscow as the fulfilment of a vow made during his return journey from Constantinople where he had been inducted; when caught in a storm on the Black Sea, he vowed that if he escaped with his life, he would found a new monastery. It bears the name of Andronik, a pupil of Sergei Radonezhsky, who became the first abbot here. The monastery, which was originally made entirely of wood, was also a fortress on the road to Vladimir. The white stone walls and towers which stand today were built during the second half of the 17th century.

In the monastery is the oldest cathedral in Moscow, the Spassky Cathedral which was built in 1420–27, but recent finds date parts of it to the 13th century. The cathedral was decorated by Andrei Rublyov, Russia's most famous icon painter, who was a monk in this monastery and who was buried here in 1430. Unfortunately all the decorations were destroyed except for fragments of the murals, believed to be the work of Rublyov, which were found around the windows which were once blocked up.

The refectory building, built of brick with a high sloping roof, was erected in 1504. In 1691–94 the Arkhangelskaya (Archangel) Church was built onto the northern and eastern walls of the refectory.

The museum, which was opened in 1960, contains a number of icons dating from the 15th to 17th centuries. Most of the icons were found in churches and monasteries in old Russian towns and have been restored. The collection is being constantly enlarged. Rublyov's work is represented by excellent copies.

**River Boat Trips

Boat trips along the river operate from May or June until September or October depending on the weather.

Route 1: From the Kiev terminal (in front of Kievsky Station) eastwards to Novospassky Bridge. This route passes Novodevichy Convent, Lenin Hills and stadium and the Kremlin. The trip lasts 1 hour 20 minutes.

Route 2: From Kiev terminal westwards to Kuntsevo-Krylatskoye. This route goes to Fili-Kuntsevo Park and the river beach. The trip lasts 1 hour.

**Market

Central Market – Tsvetnoi Boulevard. There are other big markets in Moscow too. There may be one near your hotel. They are gradually being tidied up and roofed over, but the stallholders and their produce are the same as ever. They are good places to stock up if you feel short of fresh fruit and vegetables.

**Circus

Circuses – Tsvetnoi Boulevard 13 and Prospect Vernadskogo 7. The first is under reconstruction at the time of writing.

Day 3

**Folk Art Museum

All-Russia Decorative and Folk Art Museum – Delegatskaya Street 31. Open 10–7; Tues. and Thurs. 12.30–8; closed Fri. and the last Thursday of each month. Here there is a comprehensive collection of every possible kind of craft work. There are samples of traditional lace and embroidery work, wood and bone carving, lacquer boxes, textiles, glass and metal work and in addition special exhibitions are mounted regularly to show the work of individual artists. It is a good idea to visit this museum before shopping for souvenirs and gifts; when you get to the shop you will already have seen the best and be better able to choose from what is for sale.

There is a wide variety of house-museums open in Russia. These are buildings where a famous person has lived, if only for a short time. The best are maintained as they appeared at that time, and provide fascinating glimpses into the past.

**Tolstoy's House

Tolstoy's Moscow Home – Lev Tolstoy Street 21. Open in summer 10–5; in winter 10–3.30; closed Mon. and the last Friday of each month. Sixteen rooms of this house are preserved as they were during the time that Tolstoy lived here with his family from 1882 to 1909.

**Chekhov's House

Chekhov Museum – Sadovo-Kudrinskaya Street 6.
Open 11–6; Wed. and Fri. 2–8.30; closed Mon. and the
last day of each month. Anton Chekhov, playwright
and doctor, lived here during the 1880s, and a brass
plate reading 'Dr. A.P. Chekhov' can still be seen on the
door.

**Dostoyevsky's Home

Dostoyevsky Museum – Dostoyevsky Street 2. Open
11–6; Wed. and Fri. 2–9; closed Mon., Tues. and the
last day of the month.

**Gorky's House

Kachalova Street 6/2. Open 10–6; Wed. and Fri. 12–8;
closed Mon. and Tues. The house was built in the early
20th century by F. Shekhtel, architect of the Yaroslav
Railway Terminal and the old Moscow Arts Theatre. It
is renowned for its unique architectural design and is
one of the outstanding monuments of the turn of the
century. Maxim Gorky lived here from 1931 to 1936.

**Skryabin's House

Skryabin Museum – Vakhtangov Street 11. Open
Mon., Thurs., Sun. 1–5; Tues., Fr., Sat. 3–7; closed
Wed. The well-known Russian composer and pianist
Alexander Skryabin (1871–1915) lived and died here.

**Herzen's House

Herzen Museum – Sivtsev-Vrazhek 27. Open 11–4;
Wed. and Fri. 2–9; closed Mon. and last day of each
month. The museum is dedicated to the life and work of
Alexander Herzen and is housed in his Moscow
mansion. Herzen died in Paris in 1870 but spent three
years of his life here.

Four 'Country' Estates

These four palaces have become embedded in the urban spread. They are open as museums and well worth visiting.

**Ostankino

Ostankino Palace Museum – 1–Ostankinskaya Street 5. Open 10–5 (summer); 10–3 (winter); closed Tues. and Wed.

When Count Sheremetyev inherited the Ostankino estate through his marriage with Princess Cherkasskaya in 1743 it was already one of the richest estates in Russia, having 210,000 serfs and an annual income of 1,500,000 roubles.

The palace, which is wooden although it appears to be built of stone, was built in 1792–97 by the serf architects Arguno, Mironov and Dikushin under the supervision of Quarenghi, Camporesi, Nazarov and Blank, all prominent architects of the time. The interior decoration was also the work of serfs and is particularly notable for the intricate wood-carving around the door and ceiling cornices. The parquet flooring is beautifully finished and every room has a different design, executed in various costly materials such as amaranth, rosewood and ivory.

There is a fine collection of 17th and 18th-century paintings, engravings, rare carvings, crystal, porcelain and fans.

In the 18th century the theatre in the centre of the palace was particularly renowned and its company included about 200 actors, singers, dancers and musicians. The stage is very large in comparison with the auditorium and could hold the whole company at once. At the end of a performance the armchairs in the auditorium could be removed in a matter of minutes by a special device, thus turning the theatre into a ballroom. It also had very advanced lighting, scenic and sound effects, all designed by serfs. The most popular of all the actors was a serf-actress, Parasha Kovalyova, who had been taken into the company as a girl. She came from a blacksmith's family and was admired for her beauty, great talent and goodheartedness. Count Sheremetyev fell in love with her and later married her. One of the streets in Ostankino bears her name.

When the palace was built the existing park and lands were replanned. The palace was so grand and striking in contrast to the shabby peasant huts of the nearby village that on one occasion when many guests were invited, the huts were hidden by huge screens on the top of which burning torches were placed.

On the left of the main entrance to the palace is the Trinity Church which was built in 1683 by the serf-architect Pavel Potekhin.

There is a cafe behind the palace, and two places where boats can be hired. Occasionally concerts are organised at the palace.

**Kolomenskoye

Kolomenskoye – Kashirskoye Chaussée. Open 11–5; Wed. and Thurs. in summer 1–8; closed Mon. and Tues. Kolomenskoye was once the favourite summer residence of the Grand Dukes of Moscow and later of the Russian tsars. Situated on a hill overlooking the river Moskva, the first historical record of Kolomenskoye was in 1339 when it was mentioned as the estate of Ivan Kalita. In the second half of the 17th century a large wooden palace was built and Peter the Great spent some of his childhood here. The palace was demolished in 1767 by Catherine II because it was in a state of decay. (There is a model of it in the museum.)

One of the earliest buildings still standing is the Church of the Ascension, built in old Russian 'tent' style in 1532. At the time of its construction it was the tallest church in Russia. Hector Berlioz, the French composer, wrote after a visit to Russia in the 1840s, 'Nothing has impressed me more than this relic of ancient Russian architecture in the village of Kolomenskoye.'

The Kazan Church, with five onion-shaped domes, was built in 1660. It is open for services in the mornings. The picturesque Dyakovskaya Church, built in the 16th century, served as the prototype for St. Basil's Cathedral in Moscow's Red Square.

Of the original royal estate only the Main Gate, the Clock Tower and the Water Tower are now standing.

The museum is housed in the former domestic quarters of the estate. There are exhibitions of Russian wood-carvings, metalwork, ceramics and displays illustrating the peasant war waged by Ivan Bolotnikov in 1606–07 and the 'Copper Mutiny' of 1662, so-called because of the tsar's decision that copper coins be accepted for the value of silver.

In the park are a number of wooden buildings from different parts of Russia, including the log cabin in which Peter the Great lived in Archangelsk (1702), a prison tower from Bratsk in Siberia (1631), a defence tower from the White Sea (1690), and a 17th-century mead brewery from the village of Preobrazhenskoye near Moscow.

There is an open air cafe in the park in summer.

**Kuskovo

Kuskovo Palace Museum – about 10 km (6 miles) from the centre of Moscow along the Ryazanskoye Chaussée. Open in summer 11–6; in winter 10–4; closed Mon., Tues. and the last Wednesday of each month.

First mentioned in 1510, the present architectural ensemble of Kuskovo dates from the 18th century when it was the summer residence of the Sheremetyev family, one of the oldest Russian noble families whose members were statesmen and soldiers.

The palace was built in 1769–75 by the Moscow architect Karl Blank in place of a smaller two-storey house. It was built in early Russian classical style, but is unusual for its walls of pine logs faced with painted boards. It contains about 800 *objets d'art*, including one of the best collections of 18th-century Russian art in the country. The rooms of most interest are the White Hall, the dining room, the children's room, the crimson drawing room with a large stove covered with coloured tiles, the oak-panelled study, the main bedroom and the ballroom. The 140 sq. m. of the ballroom ceiling were painted by the French artist Lagren, sen.

In front of the palace is a small square flanked by a church built in 1737 and a belfry built in 1792 by the serf-architects Mironov and Dikushin.

The park was laid out in French style under the direction of Andrei Vogt, a landscape gardener, and Yuri Kologrivov. The park which has been preserved is much smaller than the original one which included a zoo and was surrounded by woods.

There are a number of interesting buildings in the park. Near the palace is the kitchen building which was built by the serf-architect Argunov, who was also responsible for the grotto and the greenhouse. The grotto was built in 1755–61 and is faced with seashells. Beyond the grotto and behind the pond is the menagerie, reconstructed from old etchings and drawings; the pens spread out in a fan-shape running back to the semi-circle of five buildings housing the animals and birds. The greenhouse was built in 1761–65 and included a two-storey concert hall in the centre.

The Dutch house was built in 1749. The interior is decorated with pink and blue Delft tiles.

The Italian house was built in 1754–55 by Kologrivov in the style of a 17th-century Italian villa.

The Hermitage was built by Karl Blank in 1765. The statue on the cupola is of the goddess Flora. The table in the dining room on the first floor was lowered to the ground floor after each course to be cleared and reset, thereby avoiding the needs for servants to be present throughout the meal.

Also known as the State Museum of Ceramics, Kuskovo houses one of the best collections of Russian porcelain. There is also china, majolica and glass, and a considerable number of the exhibits are of Chinese, French, Dutch and English origin.

**Tsaritsyno

Tsaritsyno is about 20 km (12 miles) from the centre of town, along the Kashirskoye Chaussée, passing Kolomenskoye and the way to Domodedovo airport.

The palace of Tsaritsyno, where Catherine II intended to live as a 'simple country woman', was never completed. Work began in 1775 under Bazhenov. Ten years later and near completion, Catherine was not satisfied with it and ordered that it be pulled down. It is said that she did this to punish Bazhenov for his association with Nikolai Novikov, the eminent educator who had earned Catherine's disapproval. When work on the palace was resumed under Kazakov it was again built in the same Russian Gothic style which Bazhenov had designed. The war with Turkey and subsequent financial difficulties prevented its completion during Catherine's reign and work was stopped on her death in 1796.

Besides the half-ruined palace, one can see the Entrance Bridge and some pavilions scattered in the park. The most remarkable are the round Temple of Ceres, the Milovida Pavilion and the Ruined Tower.

Tsaritsyno is situated in one of the most beautiful

spots in Moscow, in hilly country intersected by ravines. In the English-style park there are numerous lakes and ponds. Boats can be hired and there is a cafe.

If there is time for additional excursions, those to the Yusupov palace at Arkhangelskoye, Tchaikovsky's home in Klin and Tolstoy's country house at Yasnaya Polyana are all recommended.

**Shopping

Beryozka shops accept hard currency, traveller's cheques and most credit cards. There should be better quality and selection here, and fewer shoppers, but there may be good buys in the ordinary shops too, for roubles. Posters, toys and stationery, pottery and other handicrafts.

Gastronom (groceries) – Exhibition Complex, *Krasnopresnenskaya Naberezhnaya*. Open 10–2; 3–7

Hotel Mezhdunarodnaya–2 (groceries, radio, clothing, jewellery) – *Krasnopresnenskaya Nab. 12*

Hotel Rossiya – *ulitza Razina 6*

Tsentralny Dom Turista – *Leninsky prospekt. 146*

Department Store – *Luzhnetsky proyezd 25a*. Open daily, 9 a.m.–8 p.m.

Books and Prints – *Kropotkinskaya 31*. Open 9 a.m.–8 p.m.

Gift Shop, Furs – Kutuzovsky prospekt 9. Open 10–2; 3–7

Jewellery Salon – Grokholsky pereulck 30. Open Mon.–Fri. – 9–6

Vneshtorgbank Gold Shop – *Pushkinskaya ulitza 9*. Open Mon.–Fri. 10–5

Rouble shopping:

Russian Souvenir – *Kutuzovsky prospekt 9*. Open Mon.–Sat. 11–8

Khudozhestvenny Salon (handicrafts, paintings) – *Ukrainsky Boulevard 6* and *Dmitrova Street 4*

Detsky Mir (children's department store) – *Prospect Marksa 2*. Open 8 a.m.–9 p.m.

Dom Igrushki (toys) – *Kutuzovsky Prospect 8*. Open Mon.–Sat. 11–8

**Puppet Theatre

Central Puppet Theatre – *Sadovo–Samotechnaya*. Don't miss their museum of puppets from all over the world.

Useful Information

Hotels (those with an asterisk belong to Intourist)

Aeroflot – 37 *Leningradsky prospekt*
Altai – 41 *Botanicheskaya ulitsa*
Belgrade* – 58 *Smolenskaya ulitsa*
Berlin* – 3 *Ulitsa Zhdanova*
Bucharest* – 1/15 *Sadovnicheskaya naberezhnaya*
Budapest* – 2/18 *Petrovskiye linii*
Druzhba – 53 *Prospekt Vernadskogo*
Intourist-National* – 3/5 *Ulitsa Gorkogo*
Kievskaya – 2 *Kievskaya ulitsa*
Kosmos – 150 *Prospekt Mira*
Leningradskaya – 21/40 *Kalanchovskaya ulitsa*
Metropol* – 1 *Prospekt Marksa*
Minsk – 22 *Ulitsa Gorkogo*
Mir – 9 *Bolshoi Devyatinsky pereulok*
Moskva – 7 *Prospekt Marksa*
Mozhaiskaya* – 165 *Mozhaiskoye shosse*
Ostankino – 29 *Botanicheskaya ulitsa*
Peking – 5 *Bolshaya Sadovaya ulitsa*
Rossia* – 6 *Ulitsa Razina*
Sevastopol* – 1-a *Bolshaya Yushunskaya ulitsa*
Severnaya – 50 *Sushchovsky val*
Sovietskaya – 32/2 *Leningradsky prospekt*
Sport – 90/2 *Leninsky prospekt*

contd on p. 81

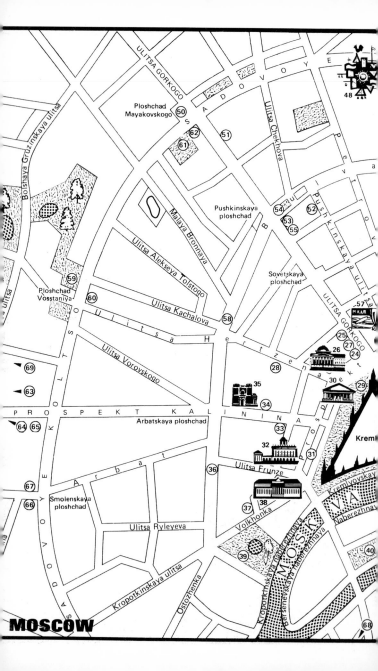

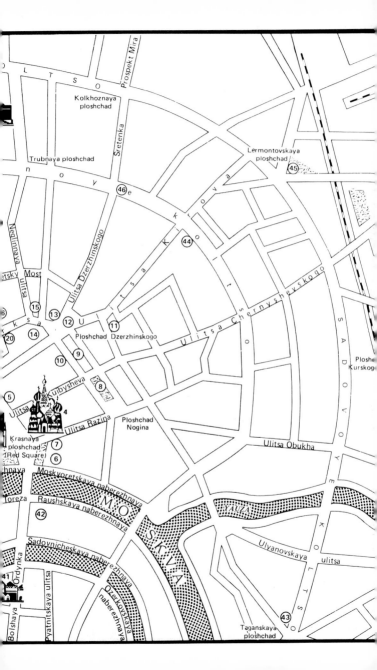

KEY TO MAP OF MOSCOW

1. Lenin Mausoleum
2. Central Lenin Museum
3. History Museum
4. Cathedral of the Intercession (St. Basil's Cathedral)
5. State Department Store (GUM)
6. Rossia Hotel
7. Palace (16th–17th cent.) in Zaryadye
8. Monument to the Russian Grenadiers
9. Polytechnical Museum
10. Museum of the History and Reconstruction of Moscow
11. Vladimir Mayakovsky Flat-Museum
12. Statue of Felix Dzerzhinsky
13. Children's World Department Store
14. Monument to Ivan Fyodorov, first Russian printer
15. Berlin Hotel
16. Maly Theatre
17. Central Department Store (TSUM)
18. Bolshoi Theatre
19. Central Children's Theatre
20. Metropol Hotel
21. Statue of Yakov Sverdlov
22. Moskva Hotel
23. House of Trade Unions
24. National Hotel
25. Yermolova Theatre
26. Moscow State University (Old Building)
27. USSR Committee for Foreign Tourism and Intourist Hotel
28. Moscow Conservatoire. Monument to Pyotr Tchaikovsky
29. Tomb of the Unknown Soldier
30. Central Exhibition Hall (Manege)
31. Mikhail Kalinin Museum
32. Lenin Library
33. Shchusev Architectural Museum
34. Monument to Mikhail Kalinin
35. Friendship House (*Dom druzhby*)
36. Monument to Nikolai Gogol
37. Karl Marx and Frederick Engels Museum
38. Pushkin Museum of Fine Arts
39. Moskva Outdoor Swimming-Pool
40. Statue of Ilya Repin
41. Tretyakov Art Gallery
42. Bucharest Hotel (refurbishing)
43. Taganka Theatre
44. Monument to Alexander Griboyedov
45. Statue of Mikhail Lermontov
46. Monument to Nadezhda Krupskaya
47. Circus (Old Building)
48. Central Puppet Theatre
49. Central Museum of the Soviet Armed Forces
50. Monument to Vladimir Mayakovsky
51. Minsk Hotel
52. Stanislavsky and Nemirovich-Danchenko Opera and Ballet Theatre
53. Nikolai Ostrovsky Flat-Museum
54. Statue of Alexander Pushkin
55. Tsentralnaya Hotel
56. Budapest Hotel
57. Moscow Art Theatre
58. Monument to Kliment Timiryazev
59. Planetarium
60. Anton Chekhov House-Museum
61. Satire Theatre
62. Tchaikovsky Concert-Hall
63. Council for Mutual Economic Assistance
64. Ukraina Hotel
65. Monument to Taras Shevchenko
66. Belgrade Hotel I
67. Belgrade Hotel II
68. Monument to Lenin
69. International Trade Centre

Sputnik – 38 *Leninsky prospekt*
Tourist – 17/2 *Selskokhozyaistvennaya ulitsa*
Tsentralnaya – 10 *Ulitsa Gorkogo*
Ukraina* – 2/1 *Kutuzovsky prospekt*
Ural – 40 *Ulitsa Chernyshevskogo*
Vostok – 9–a *Gostinichnaya ulitsa*
Warsaw – 2/1 *Leninsky prospekt*
Yaroslavskaya – 8 *Yaroslavskaya ulitsa*
Yunost – 34 *Khamovnichesky val*
Yushnaya – 87 *Leninsky prospekt*
Zarya – 5 *Gostinichnaya ulitsa*
Zolotoi Kolos – 15 *Yaroslavskaya ulitsa*

Camping

Mozhaisky – 165 *Mozhaiskoye shosse*
Solnechny – 21st km of *Varshavskoye shosse*

Museums and Exhibitions

Lenin Funeral Train Museum at the Paveletsky Railway Station (a branch of the Central Lenin Museum) – *Leninskaya ploshchad*

Krasnaya Presnya Historical-Revolutionary Museum (a branch of the Central Museum of the Revolution) – 4 *Bolshevistskaya ulitsa*

Karl Marx and Frederick Engels Museum – 5 *Ulitsa Marksa i Engelsa*

Polytechnical Museum – 3/4 *Novaya ploshchad*

Pokrovsky Sobor Museum (St. Basil's Cathedral, branch of the History Museum) – Red Square (*Krasnaya ploshchad*)

The Battle of Borodino Panorama – 38 *Kutuzovsky prospekt*

Shchusev State Research Architectural Museum
– *Prospekt Kalinina*

Novodevichy Nunnery (branch of the History
Museum) – 1 *Novodevichy proyezd*

Museum of the History and Reconstruction of
Moscow – 12 *Novaya ploshchad*

Andrei Rublyov Museum of Old Russian Art
(Andronikov Monastery) – 10 *Ploshchad
Pryamikova*

Museum of Folk Art – 7 *Ulitsa Stanislavskogo*

Housing Construction (branch of the USSR *VDNKh*)
– 30 *Frunzenskaya naberezhnaya*

Mikhail Frunze Museum of Aviation and Space
Exploration – 4 *Krasnoarmeiskaya ulitsa*

Sergei Korolyov House-Museum – 2/28 *Shestoi
Ostankinsky pereulok*

Maxim Gorky Flat-Museum – 6/2 *Ulitsa Kachalova*

Anton Chekhov House-Museum – 6 *Sadovaya-
Kudrinskaya ulitsa*

Vladimir Mayakovsky Museum – 3/6 *Proyezd Serova*

Lev Tolstoy Literary Museum – 11 *Kropotkinskaya
ulitsa*

Branch of Lev Tolstoy Museum – 12 *Pyatnitskaya
ulitsa*

Mikhail Lermontov House-Museum – 2 *Ulitsa
Malaya Molchanovka*

Alexander Ostrovsky House-Museum – 9 *Ulitsa
Ostrovskogo*

Fyodor Dostoyevsky Flat-Museum – 2 *Ulitsa
Dostoyevskogo*

Russian 18th–19th-Century Literature Museum –
28 *Petrovka*

Alexander Pushkin Museum – 12/2 *Kropotkinskaya
ulitsa*

Nikolai Ostrovsky Museum – 14 *Ulitsa Gorkogo*

Alexander Herzen Museum (branch of the Literary
Museum) – 27 *Pereulok Sivtsev-Vrazhek*

Vasily Tropinin Art Museum of Moscow Painters – 10 *Shchetininsky pereulok*

Sergei Konyonkov Memorial Studio-Museum – 28 *Tverskoi bulvar*

Victor Vaasnetsov House-Museum – 13 *Pereulok Vasnetsova*

Central Exhibition Hall – *Ploshchad Pyatidesyatiletiya Oktyabrya* (the exhibits change periodically)

Exhibition Hall of the USSR Union of Artists – 20 *Kuznetsky most*

Exhibition Hall of the USSR Academy of Arts – 21 *Kropotkinskaya ulitsa*

Sports Museum – Lenin Central Stadium (*Vostochnaya tribuna)*

Planetarium – 5 *Sadovaya-Kudrinskaya ulitsa*

Lev Tolstoy Estate-Museum – *Tulskaya oblast* (Tula region), Yasnaya Polyana (195 km from Moscow)

Abramtsevo Estate-Museum – *Yaroslavskoye shosse* (highway) (62 km from Moscow)

Theatres, Concert-Halls and the Circus

Bolshoi Theatre – *2 Ploshchad Sverdlova*

Palace of Congresses – the Kremlin, *Borovitskiye vorota*

Stanislavsky and Nemirovich-Danchenko Opera and Ballet Theatre – 17 *Pushkinskaya ulitsa*

Operetta Theatre – 6 *Pushkinskaya ulitsa*

Moscow Art Theatre – 22 *Tverskoy bulvar*
  Also – 3 *Ulitsa Moskvina*

Maly Theatre – 1/6 *Ploshchad Sverdlova*
  Branch – 69 *Bolshaya Ordynka*

Mossoviet Drama Theatre – 16 *Bolshaya Sadovaya ulitsa*

Mayakovsky Theatre – *Ulitsa Gertsena*

Central Theatre of the Soviet Army – 2 *Ploshchad Kommuny*

Vakhtangov Theatre – 26 *Arbat*

Lenin Komsomol Theatre – 6 *Ulitsa Chekhova*

Pushkin Drama Theatre – 23 *Tverskoy bulvar*

Satire Theatre – 2 *Ploshchad Mayakovskogo*

Gogol Drama Theatre 8-a *Ulitsa Kazakova*

Drama Theatre on Malaya Bronnaya – 4 *Malaya Bronnaya ulitsa*

Yermolova Theatre – 5 *Ulitsa Gorkogo*

Sovremennik Theatre – 19-a *Chistoprudny bulvar*

Taganka Theatre of Drama and Comedy – 76 *Ulitsa Chkalova*

Stanislavsky Drama Theatre – 23 *Ulitsa Gorkogo*

Roman Gipsy Theatre – 32 *Leningradsky prospekt*

Central Puppet Theatre (directed by Sergei Obraztsov) – 3 *Sadovaya-Samotyochnaya ulitsa*

Theatre for the Young – 10 *Pereulok Sadovskikh*

Central Children's Theatre – 2 *Ploshchad Sverdlova*

Moscow Puppet Theatre – 26 *Spartakovskaya ulitsa*

Children's Musical Theatre – 5 *Prospekt Vernadskogo*

Variety Theatre – 24 *Bersenevskaya naberezhnaya*

State Central Concert Hall – 1 *Moskvoretskaya naberezhnaya* (Rossia Hotel)

Tchaikovsky Concert Hall – 4 *Ploshchad Mayakovskogo*

Moscow Conservatoire (Large and Small Halls) – 13 *Ulitsa Gertsena*

House of Trade Unions (Hall of Columns) – 1/6 *Pushkinskaya ulitsa*

Oktyabr Cinema Concert Hall – 42 *Prospekt Kalinina*

Circus – 7 *Prospekt Vernadskogo*

Durov Animal Theatre – 4 *Ulitsa Durova*

Olympic Village Concert-Hall – 1 *Ulitsa Pelshe*

Mime and Gesture Theatre – 39/41 *Izmailovsky bulvar*

Restaurants

Aragvi (Georgian cuisine) – 6 *Ulitsa Gorkogo*
Arbat – 29 *Prospekt Kalinina*
Baku (Azerbaijanian cuisine) – 24/2 *Ulitsa Gorkogo*
Belgrade – 5, 8 *Smolenskaya ulitsa*
Berlin – 3 *Ulitsa Zhdanova*
Budapest – 2/18 *Petrovskiye linii*
Havana – 88 *Leninsky prospekt*
Metropol – 1 *Prospekt Marksa* (refurbishing)
Minsk (Byelorussian cuisine) – 22 *Ulitsa Gorkogo*
Moskva – 7 *Prospekt Marksa*
National – 1 *Ulitsa Gorkogo*
Pekin – 1/7 *Bolshaya Sadovaya ulitsa*
Prague – 2 *Arbat*
Rossia (Russian cuisine) – 6 *Ulitsa Razina*
Sedmoye Nebo (Ostankino TV Tower) – 15 *Ulitsa Korolyova*
Slavyansky Bazar (Russian cuisine) – 17 *Ulitsa Dvadtsat Pyatogo Oktyabrya*
Sofia (Bulgarian cuisine) – 32/1 *Ulitsa Gorkogo*
Sovetsky – 32/2 *Leningradsky prospekt*
Tsentralny – 10 *Ulitsa Gorkogo*
Ukraina (Ukrainian cuisine) – 2/1 *Kutuzovsky prospekt*
Uzbekistan (Uzbek cuisine) – 29 *Neglinnaya ulitsa*
Volga – 51 *Leningradskoye shosse*
Warsaw (Polish cuisine) – 2/1 *Oktyabrskaya ploshchad*
Zolotoi Kolos – On the grounds of the *VDNKh* (USSR Exhibition of Economic Achievement), *Prospekt Mira*
Zvezdnoye Nebo – 3/5 *Ulitsa Gorkogo*

Cooperative Restaurants in Moscow

Aist (Café) – *Malaya Bronnaya* 1/8 – 291 6692
Arevik (Café) – *Kutuzovsky Prospekt* 30/35 – 240 1528
Atrium (Café) – *Leninsky Prospekt* 44 – 137 3008

Gumista (Abkhazian Café) – *Kalyayevskaya* 29 – 258 1315

Guria (Georgian Café) – *Komsomolsky pr.* 7 – 246 0378

Kaissa (Café) – *Gogolevsky bul.* 14 – 291 0641

Kropotkinskaya-36 – *Kropotkinskaya* 36 – 201 7500

Mei-hua (Plumblossom) (Chinese) – *Rusakovskaya* 2/1 – 264 9574

Na Patriarshikh (Café) – *Mal. Bronnaya* 28

Oriental Café – *B. Polyanka* 2/10 – 238 8888

Pizzeria – *Kutuzovsky pr.* 17 – 243 7978

Pokrovka (Café) – *ul. Chernyshevskovo* 4 – 923 0282

Skazka (Café) – *Tovarischesky per.* 1 – 271 0998

Sorok Chetirye – *Leningradskoye Chaussée* 44 – 159 9951

Traktir Zamoskvorechye – *B. Polyanka* 52 – 230 7333

U Yuzefa (Jewish) – *Dubininskaya* 11 – 238 4646

U Pirosmani (Georgian) – *Novodevichyi Proyezd* 4 – 247 1926

Vitosha (Bulgarian) – *Khoroshovskoye Chaussée*, 35 – 195 4084

Vstrecha (Café) – *ul. Gilyarovskogo* 3 – 208 4597

Yakimanka (Café) – B *Polyanka* 2/10 – 238 8888

Zaidi, Poprobui ('Come and Try' Café) – *Pr. Mira* 124, Kor. 1 – 286 7503; contacting guests – 286 8165

Zarya Vostoka (Korean Café) – *ul. 26 Bakinskikh Komissarov* 4/2

Enquiries for cooperative cafés: 299 0004

Large Stores

State Department Store (GUM) – 3 *Krasnaya ploshchad*

Central Department Store (TSUM) – 2 *Petrovka*

Detsky Mir (Children's World) – *Prospekt Marksa*

Moskva Department Store – 54 *Leninsky prospekt*
Moskovsky Department Store – 6 *Komsomolskaya ploshchad*
Podarki (Presents) – 4 *Ulitsa Gorkogo*
Russky Suvenir (Russian Souvenirs) – 9 *Kutuzovsky prospekt*
Pervomaisky Department Store – 62 *Devyataya Parkovaya ulitsa*
Vanda – 30 *Ulitsa Bolshaya Polyanka*
Varna – 34 *Leninsky prospekt*
Vlasta – 82/2 *Leninsky prospekt*
Ganga – 5/23 *Smolenskaya naberezhnaya*
Sofia – 28 *Ulitsa Bolshaya Polyanka*
Polskaya moda (Polish Fashion) – 7 *Ulitsa 26 Bakinskikh Komissarov*
Budapest – 40 *Zelenodolskaya ulitsa*
Prague – 5 *Rossoshansky proyezd*
Malakhit (Malachite) – 24 *Prospekt Kalinina*
Yantar, (Amber) – 13 *Stoleshnikov pereulok*
Art Salon – 54 *Ulitsa Dimitrova*
Art Salon – 8 *Ulitsa Dvadsat Pyatogo Oktyabrya*
Moskovsky Dom knigi (Moscow House of Books) – 26 *Prospekt Kalinina*
Druzhba (books in the languages of socialist countries) – 15 *Ulitsa Gorkogo*
Knigi (Books) – 18 *Ulitsa Gorkogo*
Knizhny mir (Book World) – 6 *Ulitsa Kirova*

Major Sports Grounds

Lenin Central Stadium – *Luzhniki*
Moskva Outdoor Swimming-Pool (open all year round) – 37 *Kropotkinskaya naberezhnaya*
Dynamo Stadium and Swimming-Pool – 36 *Leningradsky prospekt*
Sokolniki Sports Palace – 1-b *Sokolnichesky val*

TsSKA (Central Sports Club of the Army) **Sports Complex** – 39 *Leningradsky prospekt*

Lokomotive Stadium 125-a *Bolshaya Cherkizovskaya ulitsa*

Brothers Znamensky Field-and-Track Stadium – 4 *Ulitsa Stromynka*

Krylya Sovetov Sports Palace – 24-a *Leningradsky prospekt*

Hippodrome – 22 *Begovaya ulitsa*

Young Pioneers' Stadium – 31 *Leningradsky prospekt*

Olympic Sports Complex – 15 *Olimpiisky prospekt*

Krylatskoye Olympic Sports Centre (bicycle tracks, archery field) – 10 *Krylatskaya ulitsa*

Krylatskoye Olympic Education and Sports Centre for Rowing (rowing canal, sports building, ski base) – 2 *Krylatskaya ulitsa*

Equestrian Sports Complex (stadium, covered manège) – 33 *Balaklavsky prospekt*

Olympic Centre for Water Sports – 27 *Mironovskaya ulitsa*

8. The River Nene and St. Andrew's Norwich

9. **The old Stock Exchange Building and the Rostral Columns**

11. The Mint, Peter and Paul Fortress

12. The Admiralty spire

13. Alexander's Column

14. Embankment of the Neva

15. Palace Square, Alexander's Column and the Hermitage

16. View along Nevsky Prospect

LENINGRAD

Here is a selection of sights to see during a three-day visit to the city. Be sure to leave yourself time just to wander through the older parts, beside the canals, over the bridges to absorb the atmosphere.

Day 1 – *Hermitage or Russian Museum, city tour, 'Aurora', Dostoyevsky Museum, canals, Kirov Ballet*

Day 2 – *Petropavlovsky Fortress, Nevsky Prospect and Kazan Cathedral, Dvortsovaya Square, the Admiralty, St. Isaac's Cathedral, boat tour on Neva from near Peter the Great monument, History of Leningrad Museum with the story of the World War II blockade or Peskaryovskoye Cemetery and War Memorial, concert hall*

Day 3 – *Menshikov Museum or Lenin Museum in the Marble Palace, Petrodvorets, Pushkino, Pavlovsk or Gatchino, white nights*

Day 1

**The Hermitage

The Hermitage Museum – Dvortsovaya Naberezhnaya 34–36.

Zimny Dvoryets (winter palace), is the oldest building on Dvortsovaya Square. It is a grandiose edifice in baroque style on the northern side of the square. It was built in 1754–64 by Rastrelli, and after the fire of 1837 was reconstructed by Stasov and Bryullov. The building is of impressive size: it contains more than 1,000 rooms and reception halls, and has 1,945 windows, 1,786 doors and 117 staircases. Many of the rooms, with their ornamentations of Russian semi-precious stones such as malachite, jasper and agate, afford unique examples of interior decoration.

Next to the palace stands the Hermitage (Ermitazh), consisting of three separate but adjoining buildings: the oldest is the so-called Small Hermitage, a two-storey pavilion which Catherine II had built by de la Mothe in 1764–67 to house her collections of paintings. It was named the Hermitage because it indeed served as a retreat for the empress from the vastness of the Winter Palace, and was a place where she could entertain artists and men of letters in more intimate surroundings than those provided by the palace. In 1775–84 another building, known as the Old Hermitage and notable for its interior decoration, was added by Felten, Director of the Imperial Academy. Here, in 1788, Quarenghi constructed the Raphael Gallery, an exact replica of the Raphael Gallery in Rome and now of particular interest as the original is in poor condition.

On the Khalturin Street side, the Old Hermitage adjoins the building of the New Hermitage, to which it is connected by a system of corridors. This was constructed in 1839–52 by the architects Klenze and

Yefimov on the orders of Nicholas I, and contains several points of interest, including the Hall of Twenty Columns, with pillars of Karelian granite, and the white marble Roman courtyard. Its portico is supported by granite figures of the Atlantes.

These buildings house Leningrad's world-famous collections of paintings and other priceless art treasures. The State Hermitage contains one of the largest and most valuable collections of paintings in the world, including priceless examples of works by the greatest Western European masters. Although it is often claimed that Catherine II was the real creator of the Hermitage collections, several paintings which hang here today were in fact purchased earlier, in the reign of Peter the Great. Peter's interest in art was mainly of a practical nature; in particular he recognised the value of art as a propaganda instrument in his struggle for the modernisation of Russia, and this explains his predilection for the work of such Dutch painters as Adam Silo which depicts the ships and shipyards of the Netherlands. However, we also know that in 1716 Peter purchased for the Hermitage one of its Rembrandts, 'David's Farewell to Jonathan'. Peter also began collections of Russian antiquities by issuing an order prescribing the careful preservation of all ancient objects found in the ground; as a result we have the Siberian collection, mainly of gold objects, to be seen in the Hermitage today.

It was Catherine II, however, who began collecting art, mainly Western art, for its own sake, on a large scale. She systematically bought up whole collections of paintings, such as that of Gotkowski, which comprised 225 pictures, including several Rembrandts, a Frans Hals, a Van der Helst, and two Gotzius. Her ambassadors throughout Europe, and particularly in Paris, were ordered to keep her constantly informed of interesting sales, and in 1769 she pulled off a major *coup* by acquiring for 180,000 roubles the collection of the recently deceased Count de Bruhl of Dresden. This contained many masterpieces: 4 paintings by Rembrandt, 4 Ruisdaels, 21 Wouwermans, 5 Rubens and several Bellottos and Watteaus. One of the most remarkable collections in Europe was that of Sir Robert Walpole, which was sold to Catherine by his grandson, Horace Walpole. The loss to the British nation was appreciated all too late, and it was then decided that a national collection should be formed. It was Catherine too who had the actual buildings of the Hermitage constructed to house her collections of paintings, and so many were the pictures she purchased that the high walls were closely covered from the floor to the ceiling. On Catherine's death it was estimated that the imperial collections totalled 3,926 pictures.

The process of collecting was continued, to a greater or lesser degree, by succeeding monarchs; in particular Nicholas I greatly expanded the collection, and did much to rectify the preponderance of Dutch and Flemish paintings by purchasing works of the Spanish and Italian schools. Hitherto the collection had been an entirely private one, open only to a few privileged guests and visitors. It was Nicholas I who, in 1852, opened the Hermitage as a public museum, and from this time the Hermitage became an independent administration under the direction of curators; now the acquisition of paintings no longer depended as before on the individual caprices of the tsar, but on the decisions of a public body. Apart from works purchased abroad, the Hermitage also benefited to a large extent from the collections of members of the Russian aristocracy who, following the fashion set by Catherine II, had become prodigious collectors of Western art. After the Revolution the private collections which remained in Russia, such as those of the Stroganov and

Yusupov families, were all taken over by the State and went to swell the Hermitage collection. Thanks to such discriminating collectors as Sergei Shchukin and Ivan Morozov, who both purchased and also commissioned works from contemporary artists such as Bonnard, Cezanne, Picasso and Matisse, the Hermitage still has one of the world's richest collections of Impressionist art, even though several of these paintings have now been transferred to the Pushkin Museum in Moscow.

**Russian Museum
Ingenernaya Street 4/2.

The Russian Museum is also housed in a striking building. The large Mikhailovsky Dvoryets (palace) was built in 1819–25 by Rossi for Nicholas I's brother, the Grand Duke Michael. The State Russian Museum is the second largest depository of Russian art after the Tretyakov Gallery in Moscow. It has about 300,000 exhibits in all, dating from the 10th century to the present day. They include priceless specimens of Russian 12th and 13th century icon painting by Rublyov and Ushakov, and works by such well-known 18th and 19th century artists as Ivanov, Levitan, Repin and Bryullov.

**A Tour of the City
A tour of the city of Leningrad will help to give a feel of the spread of this Venice of the North, with its islands and bridges and numerous interconnecting waterways. From the beginning the city layout conformed to strict planning under the personal direction of Peter I. Even today his planning is evident for, on the left side of the river, the three main streets converge upon the golden-spired building of the Admiralty where the first shipyard used to be, while a series of canals form concentric semi-circles around it, flowing into the river on either side. The right bank of the main stream of the

river is at this point formed by many islands. Spreading behind the Peter and Paul Fortress is Petrogradskaya Storona and nearer the sea is the expanse of Vasilyevsky Ostrov (island).

**'Aurora'

The 'Aurora' – Petrogradskaya Naberezhnaya 4.

The cruiser 'Aurora' is moored in the Neva near the Nakhimov Naval College. This ship fired a blank shot as the signal for assault on the Winter Palace on 7th November (24th October) 1917, the day kept annually as the Day of the October Socialist Revolution. The ship was built in 1900 and took part in the Russo-Japanese War of 1904–05. The gun which fired the shot and the radio room from which Lenin's manifesto announcing the victory of the revolution was transmitted are still to be seen, and the ship is open to the public.

**Dostoyevsky's Flat

Dostoyevsky Museum – Kuznechny Pereulok 5/2 (just behind Kuznetsky Market). In spite of the rather unprepossessing entrance, the museum has a rich collection of documents on the first floor while the flat where the writer lived and worked is on the second.

**Canals

Although visitors find themselves constantly crossing the canals on their bus tour, a walk along the banks of the Fontanka, the Griboyedov Canal and the little river Moika give a very different impression of these waterways. Peter the Great had Amsterdam in mind when he drew up the plans for the layout of his city, but there was never the bustle of Dutch trading here and the embankments breathe an air of aristocratic reserve.

**Kirov Theatre

Kirov Opera and Ballet Theatre – Teatralnaya Square 1.

The building of the Kirov State Theatre of Opera and Ballet was formerly called the Mariinsky Theatre in honour of the Tsaritsa Maria, wife of Alexander II. Designed by the architect Kavos in 1860, this theatre was one of the most important centres of Russian opera and ballet. Both Fyodor Chaliapin and Anna Pavlova performed here.

Day 2

**Petropavlovskaya Fortress

Petropavlovskaya (Peter and Paul) Fortress – Zayachy Island.

In 1706 builders began to replace the original earthworks, founded in 1703, with powerful brick fortifications 12 m (40 ft) high; the task was not completed, however, for 35 years, and later the walls were faced with granite slabs. Gradually the fortress lost its military importance and became a prison. The first prisoner held there was Peter I's son, Alexei, who was tortured to death on his father's orders in 1718. From the end of the 18th century the fortress served as a prison for political offenders. In 1924 it was opened as a museum.

The fortress is entered through the outer Ioanovskiye Vorota (the John Gate) and the Petrovskiye Vorota (the Peter Gate). The latter is of particular interest, as it is the only building in the fortress that has remained practically unchanged since it was first built. It was designed by Domenico Trezzini, built 1717–18, and adorned with bas-reliefs by Konrad Osner representing the story of Peter confounding Simon the Sorcerer. In the niches are statues of Mars and Venus. In the centre of the fortress stands the Petropavlovsky Sobor (Peter and Paul Cathedral). This is a domed building, in Dutch style, and was erected between 1712 and 1721, also by Trezzini. It was reconstructed by Rastrelli and Chevakinsky in 1750 after a fire, and again altered under Nicholas I. It is 64 m (70 yds) long and 30 m (33 yds) wide; the extremely slender gilded spire, which stands 120 m (394 ft) high, is crowned by an angel bearing a cross, the work of Rinaldi. The clock in the tower was brought from Cologne in 1760. Of particular interest inside the cathedral are the pulpit, rare in a Russian church, dating from the time of Peter the Great, and the carved and gilded wooden iconostasis made in the 1720s. This cathedral is the burial place of all the Russian tsars, from Peter I to Alexander III, with the exception of Peter II. The imperial tombs are of white marble, with gilded eagles at the corners. The sarcophagi of Alexander II and his wife, however, are carved respectively of Altai jasper and red Ural quartz; the work on these tombs took 17 years.

To the west, opposite the cathedral, is Monetny Dvor (the Mint). This was originally founded in 1724, but the present building by Voronikhin dates from the 19th century.

Also near the Fortress Cathedral stands the Nevskiye Vorota (the Neva Gate), built by Lvov in 1787. It was through this gate that prisoners were led out to the gallows.

**Nevsky Prospect

This is the main street of the city and one of the oldest. It was built in 1710 to link the Admiralty Yard directly with the Great Novgorod Road leading to Novgorod. Beginning at the Admiralty building, it runs to the Moscow Railway Station and then stretches on further to the Alexander Nevsky Lavra (Monastery), covering a total of 4.5 km (2.5 miles).

Here, in tsarist times, were built all the largest banks, the best shops and the palaces of the nobility. House No. 9, on the corner of Gogol Street, was once the Wavelburg Bank, built in 1912 by Petryatkovich in imitation of the Doge's Palace in Venice and the Medici Palace in Florence. In Gogol Street, house No. 13 was for a long time the residence of the composer Tchaikovsky, who died there on 25 October 1893. No. 17 was occupied by the writer Gogol from 1833–6.

The next side-road is Herzen Street. The part of Herzen Street to the north of Nevsky Prospect was built by the architect Rossi straight along the Pulkovo meridian, and at noon on a sunny day one can check one's watch by it – the facades of the houses cast no shade.

No. 15 Nevsky Prospect is one of the oldest in the street. It was built in 1768–71 by Kokorinov for the chief of the St. Petersburg police, Chicherin, and is now a cinema. The elegant classical building at No. 20 was once the Dutch Church built in 1837 by Jacquot, and is now a library.

On the corner of the Moika Embankment is the white-columned Stroganov Dvoryets (palace), built in 1752–4 by the architect Rastrelli, and one of the best examples of Russian baroque.

**Kazan Cathedral

No. 22–24 is the former Lutheran Church of SS. Peter and Paul, built in Romanesque style by the architect Bryullov in 1833–8. Almost opposite stands the impressive Kazan Cathedral, which is approached by a semi-circular colonnade of 136 Corinthian columns, modelled on that of St. Peter's in Rome. It was designed by Andrei Voronikhin (1760–1814) and at the time of its construction in 1811 was the third largest cathedral in the world. It is 79 m (259 ft) high, 72 m (79 yds) long and 55 m (60 yds) wide, built in the shape of a Latin cross in Greek neo-classical style. Huge bas-reliefs on biblical themes adorn the end walls of the colonnade, and the niches of the facade contain enormous statues of Russian warriors. The small square in front of the main entrance is surrounded by beautiful ironwork, also designed by Voronikhin. To the right of the entrance is the tomb of Field Marshal Kutuzov, and on either side hang the keys of the towns and cities he captured during his campaigns. Nearby is a memorial to the architect of the cathedral. The building takes its name from the wonder-working icon of Our Lady of Kazan, which used to be here but has now been transferred to the Russian Museum. It is worth-while going down into the crypt to see the exhibits there. The cathedral is no longer open for services, but houses the Museum of the History of Religion and Atheism.

In the square in front of the Cathedral stand statues, designed by Orlovsky in 1831–32, of Kutuzov and of General Barclay de Tolly, who led the Russian army to victory in the 1812 campaign. At their feet lie the banners of Napoleon's defeated army.

On the corner of Nevsky Prospect and the Griboyedov Canal stands a building faced with polished granite, with a glass tower and a 3 m (10 ft) glass globe, which was built in 1907 and formerly belonged to the Singer sewing-machine company.

On the left, some distance along the embankment, stands a church built in 1883–1907 by Parland on the spot where in 1881 Alexander II was assassinated by members of the Narodnaya Volya (People's Freedom) group. The church is in the old Russian style, with ornate decorations, and was modelled on St. Basil's Cathedral in Moscow. It is called the Church of the Resurrection.

No. 30 Nevsky Prospect was once owned by a friend of Pushkin's, Engelhardt, and later, in the 19th century, was used for concerts by the Philharmonic Society. Performers there included Berlioz, Wagner, Liszt, and Strauss. Today it is the Small Hall of the Leningrad State Philharmonic Society. Next door (Nos. 32–34), was formerly the Roman Catholic Church of St. Catherine, built by de la Mothe in 1763–4 in the shape of a Latin cross. The pentagonal tower by Ferrari (1802) was used originally as a firemen's watch-tower, then as a semaphore station linking St. Petersburg with such country residences as Tsarskoye Selo. There was even a connection with Warsaw; from the Winter Palace a series of 149 such towers, all of them over 15 m (49 ft) high, passed messages between the Polish and the Russian capitals.

At this point on Nevsky the side-street to the left, Brodsky street, links Nevsky Prospect with Iskusstv (arts) Square where the Russian Museum stands.

Back on Nevsky Prospect, No. 35 is the 230 m (252-yd) frontage of Gostiny Dvor department store, a two-storey building with a row of arches and arcades along each floor. It was built in 1761–85 by de la Mothe, and numerous shops were built into galleries forming a square, 1 km (0.6 miles) around. The interior has now been reconstructed to form the largest department store in the city. Opposite, at Nos. 40–2, is the small but elegant former Armenian Church built in the 1770s, probably by Felten, and a little further down is another big arcade of shops founded in 1848 and reconstructed in 1900, now turned into another large department store.

At the corner of Sadovaya Street is the Saltykov-Shchedrin Library, built partly by Sokolov in 1796–1801 and partly by Rossi in 1828–32 and decorated with bas-reliefs and carvings of orators, philosophers, and writers of ancient times. It is one of the largest libraries in the world.

**Rossi Street

At this point Nevsky Prospect runs into Ostrovsky Square, on the south side of which stands the Pushkin Drama Theatre. It was built by Rossi in 1832 and, until the revolution, it was called the Alexandrinsky Theatre in honour of Tsaritsa Alexandra, wife of Nicholas I. Southwards from the theatre runs an interesting street name after Rossi, who designed it in 1828–34. On either side lie identical buildings, painted yellow and decorated with white columns, whose walls are exactly the same height as the width of the street. The length of the street is exactly ten times its width. In the centre of the gardens in Ostrovsky Square stands a statue of Catherine II, erected in 1873 by Mikyeshin. Round the base of the statue are grouped figures of the distinguished from 18th-century Russia. On the eastern side of the square stands the Anichkov Dvoryets, built in 1741–7 to the designs of Rastrelli, by order of the Empress Elizabeth for her favourite, Count Razumovsky.

**Anichkov Bridge

At the point where Nevsky Prospect crosses the Fontanka is the famous Anichkov Most (bridge). The present bridge was built in 1838–41, with railings designed by Montferrand. It is chiefly noted for its statues of youths with horses by Peter Klodt; these were begun 10 years before the present bridge was completed. Originally there were two statues, each cast twice and placed at the four corners of the bridge. Then one pair was sent by Nicholas I to the King of Prussia as a present and plaster casts, painted in imitation of bronze, were erected in their place. New casts were made, but in 1846 Nicholas again sent them away as a present, this time to the King of Sicily. In 1850 Klodt made two different statues to complete the set, and they were eventually erected on the bridge. They have stood here since then, except for a time during World War II, when they were buried in the nearby gardens for protection.

The rest of Nevsky Prospect, from the Fontanka to Vosstaniya (uprising) Square, was built mainly at the end of the 19th century, and there is little of very great architectural interest here. In Vosstaniya Square stands the Moscow Railway Station building designed by Thon and opened in 1851 when trains started running between St. Petersburg and Moscow.

**Dvortsovaya Square

Back at the other end of Nevsky Prospect, the last side street on the right, facing the Admiralty, looks rather unprepossessing. It ends with an arch, and the bend in that archway keeps the secret of what lies ahead. Quite suddenly the whole expanse of Dvortsovaya (Palace) Square opens out.

At the beginning of the 19th century the government decided to make Palace Square into one complete architectural unit, and therefore bought up all the private buildings on the south side. In 1819 Carl Rossi was commissioned to design an administrative building, the Glavny Shtab (General Headquarters), and the result was a severe classical building, almost totally devoid of decoration, completed in 1829. At one time it housed the offices of the Ministries of Finance and Foreign Affairs. The horseshoe-shaped facade centres on the Winter Palace and is broken by a large archway. This triumphal arch is surmounted by a bronze six-horse victory chariot by Pimenov and Demut-Malinovsky, symbolising the victory of Russia over Napoleon in 1812. The 28 m (92 ft) arch is further decorated with coats-of-arms and martial figures, and is now called the Triumphal Arch of the Red Army.

In the centre of the square stands a triumphal column, Alexandrovskaya Kolonna (Alexander's Column), which also commemorates the Russian victory in the war of 1812. It was designed by Montferrand and erected in 1834 on the orders of Nicholas I in memory of Alexander I, and it bears the inscriptions, 'To Alexander I from a Grateful Russia'. The column of polished red Finnish granite stands 30 m (98 ft) high, weighs 600 tons and was quarried out of a cliff in the Gulf of Finland, a task which took three years. It was brought to St. Petersburg on a specially constructed barge, and it took 2000 soldiers, aided by a complicated system of pulleys, to raise it into position. After erection, the column was given its final polishing and crowned with the huge figure of an angel by Orlovsky representing the peace that was established in Europe after the victory over Napoleon.

On the eastern side of the square are former barracks, built in 1840 by Bryullov for one of the Guards regiments.

To the west of the Winter Palace lies the huge building of the Admiralty. This was founded originally in 1704 by Peter the Great as a fortress and shipyard. The present building, in a broad U-shape, dates from the years 1806–23. Over the gateway rises the Admiralty Tower, visible from almost all parts of the city. It is 70 m (230 ft) high, ending in a tapering, gilded spire and surmounted by a weathervane in the form of a crown and ship.

**Peter the Great Statue

From the west wing of the Admiralty stretches Ploshchad Dekabristov (Decembrists' Square), which takes its name from the conspirators, mainly tsarist officers, who in December 1825 attempted a *coup d'état* and gathered here outside the Senate and the Council of State. In the centre of this grassy square stands the celebrated Peter the Great Monument, the work of French sculptor Etien Falconet, unveiled in 1782. Pushkin, in his poem The Bronze Horseman, wrote of it:

> There by the billows desolate
> He stood, with mighty thoughts elate,
> And gazed.

The enormous solid block of granite which forms the pedestal weighs nearly 1,500 tons and was transported part of the way to St. Petersburg on an ingeniously constructed platform running on wheels.

On the opposite side of the square to the Admiralty stand the twin buildings of the former Senate and the Holy Synod. The Senate House was designed in 1763; in 1829–34 it and the Synod were reconstructed by Rossi and connected by a gallery spanning the street between them. In the south-west corner of the square stands a former manège, or riding school, built by Quarenghi in 1804–7 and decorated with marble figures.

**St. Isaac's

To the south of the square stands the magnificent structure of Leningrad's largest church, St. Isaac's Cathedral. This, with its impressive columned porticos, beautiful bronze sculpture and golden dome, took the French architect Auguste Montferrand over forty years (1819–59) to build. He was assisted by Elson, responsible also for Prince Golitsyn's Crimean palace at Gaspra. Constructed of granite and marble, in the shape of a cross, it is 111 m (121 yds) long, 96 m (105 yds) wide and has a total height of 110 m (361 ft). The enormous dome is visible from afar, and there is a magnificent view of the city and the river from here. (Permission is needed to take photographs). The building, which can hold 14,000 people, is open now as a museum.

**River Boat Trip

Boat Trip on the Neva

Boats leave from the quay near Peter the Great statue and afford another view of the spectacular Leningrad skyline.

**History of Leningrad Museum

History of Leningrad Museum – Naberezhnaya Krasnovo Flota 44. Open 11–6; closed Wed.

The museum building, designed by Glinka in 1826, first belonged to an English merchant, but was then purchased by Count Rumyantsev (son of the field marshal). The exhibits here include the story of the 1941–43 defence of the city, the blockade when its survival depended upon the maintenance of the tenuous supply lines, and the final collapse of the blockade when the Soviet Army cut through south of Schusselburg.

**Piskaryovskoye Cemetery

Piskaryovskoye Memorial Cemetery – Nepokorennykh Prospect 9.

In 1941 this cemetery became the burial ground for the civilians and soldiers who numbered among Leningrad's war dead during the blockade. Two pavilions at the entrance contain museum material, and beyond an eternal flame overlooks the rows of nameless gravestones. The memorial complex includes bas-reliefs symbolising Leningrad's struggle for survival and a monumental figure of the Motherland. It was completed in 1960.

**Concert Hall

Philharmonic Society, Large Hall – Brodsky Street 2.

This is a very beautiful concert hall, a treat to come to at the end of a long day.

Day 3

**Menshikov's Palace

Menshikov's Palace – Universitetskaya Naberezhnaya. Open 10.30-6; closed Mon. Intourist arranges tours for groups of limited size; tickets should be obtained in advance.

The three-storey, red and white building of the Menshikov Palace stands near the university. It was built as the first stone structure in St. Petersburg by the architects Giovanni Fontana and Schedel for General Alexander Menshikov (1670–1729) in 1707, when Peter the Great presented the whole of Vasilyevsky Ostrov to him so that he could build a residence there. Menshikov was his close friend and comrade-in-arms, and first governor-general of St. Petersburg, and indeed second in importance only to the tsar. The building was relatively small and homely, and Peter himself was very fond of visiting there. Guests arrived by boat, and from the riverside they climbed an oak stairway that led to the great hall. From the window of the hall there is a beautiful view over the Neva. Menshikov had a splendid gilded gondola which never failed to catch the eye of passers-by. (The gift was withdrawn again, however, in 1714.)

From 1732 the building was used as a military school and a long, new wing was added. The original Dutch tiles which line a number of the rooms were covered with layers of plaster and paint, and were thus preserved intact until their recent discovery. The interiors all date from the early 18th century and have been carefully restored to their original appearance. The floors are excellent examples of early parquet, and in the room that belonged to Menshikov's wife is an oval English table made of a single piece of fine wood. The rest of the furniture also dates from the early 18th century, and many pieces were previously in the Hermitage Museum to which this is now affiliated. In the Shpalernaya Room hang valuable tapestries with scenes from the Odyssey. This museum is well worth a visit for its 18th century interiors alone, not to mention its historical importance.

**Lenin Museum

Lenin Museum – Khalturin Street 5/1. Open 10.30–6.30; closed Wed.

Standing on the north-west corner of the Field of Mars is Mramorny Dvoryets (marble palace), built in 1768–85 from plans by Antonio Rinaldi and presented by Catherine II to Count Orlov. Thirty-two kinds of marble were used for the facing and the interior decoration of the palace.

**Petrodvorets

Comintern Street 2.

Can be reached by road or by boat from Leningrad. It is about 34 km (21 miles) from Leningrad on the low, southern shore of the Gulf of Finland. The buildings are open 10.30–5; closed Mon. and the last Tuesday of each month.

Petrodvorets was founded by Peter the Great, who gave it the German name Peterhof, in commemoration of the victory of the Russian army over the Swedes at Poltava and the gaining of an outlet to the Baltic.

Petrodvorets is mainly famous for its system of fountains which begins 21 km (13 miles) away on the Ropshinskiye Heights. It was Peter the Great's intention to make Petrodvorets the Russian equivalent of Versailles; he himself drafted the original layout of the park and gave numerous instructions on the decoration of the pavilions and the design of the fountains. Over 4,000 soldiers and peasants dug canals for the fountains which altogether use nearly 30,000 litres (7,500 gallons) of water each second. The system was designed by hydro-engineer Tuvolkov, and the water supply is sufficient to enable the fountains to work 10–12 hours out of every 24.

The Grand Palace was begun in 1715–24 according to plans by Le Blond, but its modest dimensions could not hold the large imperial court. It was reconstructed and enlarged for the Tsaritsa Elizabeth by Rastrelli in 1746–51. The main building has three storeys and is connected to the wings by galleries. The facade is 268 m (293 yds) long and at the eastern corner of the palace is a church built in Rococo style with five gilded cupolas by Rastrelli in 1751. These buildings were burned down during World War II and are under reconstruction, the work proceeding in accordance with drawings, photographs, and other documents so that the reconstructed ensemble will be as like the original as possible. The grounds also suffered during the war when 25,000 trees were felled.

The Grand Palace stands on a terrace about 12 m (39 ft) high. The surrounding park and gardens cover approximately 120 hectares (300 acres). From the grounds in front of the palace there is a wonderful view of the Nizhny (Lower) Park which stretches between the ridge of hills in the background and the shore of the Gulf of Finland. The facade of the palace facing the sea towers over the Grand Cascade, a great system of fountains which descends in broad steps to the park below. The most famous of the 129 fountains now operative is directly in front of the palace facade, at the head of the Grand Cascade; this is the Samson Fountain, where Samson is portrayed tearing open the jaws of a lion from which a jet of water rises 20 m (66 ft) into the air. The lion represents Sweden defeated by Russia at the Battle of Poltava on St. Samson's Day in 1709. Other sights of interest include the Chessboard Cascade, and the Zontik (little umbrella) and Dubok (little oak) surprise fountains which shower any unsuspecting visitors who come near.

The Hermitage is a two-storey pavilion built for Peter the Great. The walls of the dining room on the first floor are lined with Dutch paintings, and part of the table can sink to the floor below to be cleared and relaid. To the right of the Hermitage is a statue of Peter, made by Antokolsky in 1883.

The small villa in Dutch style, built in the early 18th century, where Peter the Great lived while the Grand Palace was under construction, is known as Mon Plaisir. The stone wing of this miniature palace was built by Rastrelli and reconstructed by Quarenghi, and inside it is decorated with numerous paintings. The Dutch-style garden contains small flowerbeds and exotic trees. Marly is the name of the small two-storey house in Louis XIV style built in 1714 by Peter the Great.

The pavilions which stand on either side of the canal were designed by Voronikhin in about 1800.

**Pushkin

PUSHKIN, Komsomolskaya Street 7; 27 km (17 miles) south of Leningrad. Visitors can also reach Pushkin by train from Vitebsky Station in Leningrad. There are buses and taxis from the station to Yekaterininsky Palace which is open 10–5; closed Tues. and the last Monday of each month.

Formerly Tsarskoye Selo (Tsar's Village), the place was called Detskoye Selo (Childrens' Village) after the revolution because the buildings were used as kindergartens, children's hospitals, sanatoria and schools. In 1937 it was again renamed, this time after Alexander Pushkin on the occasion of the 100th anniversary of the poet's death.

The so-called Egyptian Gates mark the entrance to the village. They were designed by the English architect, Adam Menelaws, and built in 1828; Menelaws also built a ruined 'chapel' and a Turkish style elephant house for the zoo. By the Egyptian Gates stands a monument to Pushkin (1911) by Bernstam.

Yekaterininsky Palace was built during the reigns of Elizabeth, the youngest daughter of Peter the Great, and Catherine II. It takes its name from the wife of Peter the Great, Catherine I, to whom the village was given by her husband. The small two-storey palace which was first built here in the reign of Peter was later incorporated into the main palace.

The palace was begun by the architects Kvasov and Chevakinsky, and completed by Rastrelli. With its azure facade over 300 m (328 yds) long and gold ornamentation and ornate pilasters and sculptures, it is one of the finest examples of Russian baroque architecture. It was badly burnt during the Second World War, but has since been restored in accordance with the original plans.

Part of the palace is now open as a museum. In a number of halls which have not yet been completely restored there is an exhibition relating the history of the palace, of its furniture and china. Other halls which have been completely restored and which are open include the Green Dining-Room, the Light Blue Parlour, and the Chinese Light Blue Parlour. The Amber Room, in which all the decorations were of amber, was completely gutted by the Nazi troops during the war, and the decorations have never been found. It is thought possible that the amber still lies under the ruins of Kaliningrad, then Konisberg. The Hall of Paintings contains 130 paintings, 114 of which were in the palace collection before the Second World War.

In the former Church Wing of the palace is the

Pushkin Museum which contains over 700 pages of the poet's manuscripts as well as a number of his personal belongings, rare books, a collection of portraits painted during his lifetime, and several portraits of his contemporaries.

Yekaterininsky Park covers 592 hectares (1,482 acres). The land was given to Catherine I by her husband, Peter the Great, and subsequently gardens, a hothouse, ponds and a zoo were laid out. The gardens were developed in the course of fifty years and include many buildings of different styles. An obelisk, unveiled in 1771, commemorates the Russian victory over the Turks near the Danube. The Orlov Column, on an island in the middle of the lake, was erected in 1778 by Rinaldi to commemorate Prince Orlov's victory at Chesma; this was a sea battle where the Russians again beat the Turks.

Cameron's Gallery, built in 1779–93 by the Scottish architect Charles Cameron, is adorned with busts of Greek and Roman philosophers. The Grotto was designed by Rastrelli who, together with Chevakinsky, was also responsible for the Concert Hall on the island. The Hermitage was built in 1744 by Kvasov and completed in 1759 by Rastrelli. It was used as a place for relaxation by the imperial family. The fantastically carved facade is decorated with 64 columns and a mass of ornamentation. The ingenious cross-shaped layout of the building fits well into the surrounding gardens.

The Agate Rooms, a two-storey building so named because of the interior which was fitted out by Cameron with jasper and marble to give the effect of agate, is being restored. The upper floor of the building is open in summer. Both the Agate Rooms and the Hermitage were used as stables by the enemy during the Second World War.

Also open is the Upper Bath House which was built in 1777–9 by Neyelov and used by the imperial family.

The Lower Bath House, built at the same time, was used by courtiers. The Marble Bridge was designed in 1770–6, also by Neyelov, and built from Siberian marble which was carved in Siberia and transported here ready for erection.

Alexander I's Triumphal Arch was built by Stasov in 1817–21 in honour of the Russian victory of 1812.

Vecherny Zal (Evening Hall) near Yekaterininsky Palace was designed by Neyelov in 1796–1810.

The Granite Terrace was planned by Luigi Rusca in 1809.

The bronze fountain, 'Girl with a Pitcher', was made by Sokolov in 1810. It was mentioned by Pushkin in one of his poems.

The Alexandrovsky Palace was built by Quarenghi in 1792–6 for Alexander I, grandson of Catherine II. Nicholas II lived here almost permanently after the 1905 revolution. The palace is not open to the public. In the Alexandrovsky Park are the Ruined Kitchen (built of real pieces of ancient ruins brought from Italy), many chinoiseries (including the Chinese village and the Chinese summer-house) and the Grande Caprice built by Neyelov in 1770–3.

The Lycée is linked to the Yekaterininsky Palace by an arch over the road. Neyelov erected the building in 1791, and a school for the nobility was opened here in 1811; Alexander Pushkin, who spent his schooldays here, was one of the first pupils. The school moved to Kirovsky Prospect in Leningrad in 1843, after which time it was known as the Alexandrovsky Lycée. The garden was relaid under the direction of the architect Stasov at the beginning of the 19th century. The monument to Pushkin was made by Bakh in 1909. The Lycée building is open from 11–6, closed Tues.

By the Lycée is Znamenskaya Church, built in 1734–47 by the Moscow architect Karl Blank and the first stone building in the village.

**Pavlovsk

Revolutsii Street 20; 35 km (22 miles) south of
Leningrad and 3 km (2 miles) from Pushkin. The
entrance to the town on the road from Pushkin is
marked by cast-iron gates designed by Rossi in 1826.
Visitors to the palace, which is open from 10.30–5.30
(closed Fri. and the first Monday of each month),
should leave their cars by the wooden bridge; it is a
short walk across the bridge and up the drive to the
palace itself.

This territory was originally hunting ground
attached to the imperial estate of Tsarskoye Selo, 3 km
(2 miles) away. In 1777 Catherine II gave the land,
including two villages and their serfs, to her son Paul
as a site for a country residence, and they then received
the name of Pavlovskoye, Paul's Village.

The Scottish architect Charles Cameron, who was
invited to Russia by Catherine II, was responsible for
the original planning of Pavlovsk, which is one of the
finest palaces in Russia. The Grand Palace was later
enlarged and decorated inside by Voronikhin,
Quarenghi, Brenna and Rossi.

It now has three storeys and a central dome which
rests on 64 columns.

The palace was badly damaged during the Second
World War, but it has since been restored according to
the original plans. The statue of Paul I in the middle of
the main courtyard was designed by Klodt in 1872.

Four halls on the ground floor, the ballroom, drawing
room, billiard room, and dining room, have been
restored according to Cameron's designs. All the rooms
on the first floor, which is approached through the
Egyptian vestibule, were built for receptions and were
never in daily use. They now contain a fine collection of
paintings, furniture and china. The collection of
antique sculptures is one of the largest after the

Hermitage in Leningrad. Many of the these were bought by Catherine from the British collector, Lord Hamilton. All the furniture in the Greek Hall was carried by hand from St. Petersburg by soldiers during the reign of Paul I.

In twelve halls on the third floor is a permanent exhibition of Russian costumes and portraits of the 18th and 19th centuries. The collection of paintings is based on the palace collection which was removed from the palace during the Second World War.

Cameron was also responsible for the first plans of the surrounding park; with 600 hectares (1,500 acres), it is one of the largest landscaped parks in Europe. The river Slavyanka was dammed to form a lake, and the trees were planted with special attention to their autumn colours. The park is intersected by avenues and winding paths which lead to pavilions and statues, and which constantly reveal new views of the beautifully landscaped estate. Unlike Petrodvorets, where the fountains and other objects of interest are so arranged that they can easily be seen from afar, the architectural sights of Pavlovsk are mostly cleverly concealed in the park in order to afford a series of surprises.

At the end of the 18th century the park was extended, mainly by the architect Brenna. The sections which were added under his direction were the Old Sylvia and the New Sylvia, to the north-west of the palace. In the New Sylvia (furthest from the palace) is the Paul I Mausoleum, a pavilion in the form of an ancient temple. It was never used as a burial place and its function is purely decorative. It was built in 1807–8 by the architect Thomas de Thomon with sculptures by Martos.

Adjoining the palace, between the lime avenue and the Slavyanka valley is a section called the Grand Circles, which takes its name from two large circular

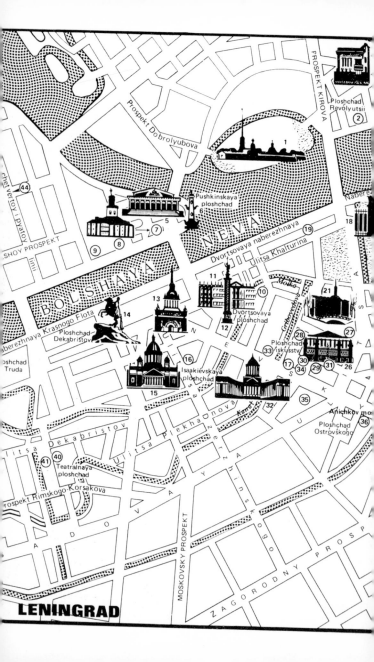

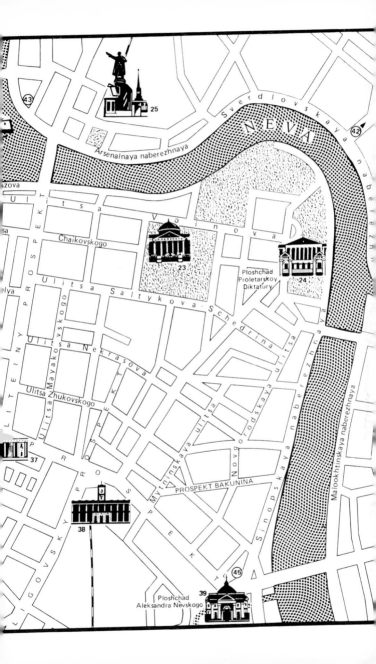

43

25

Sverdlovskaya naberezhn

42

NEVA

Arsenalnaya naberezhnaya

azova

Ulitsa

sa

Chaikovskogo

V
o
r
o
n
o
v
a

23

Ploshchad
Proletarskoy
Diktatury

24

elya

Ulitsa Saltykova-Schedrina

L
I
T
E
I
N
Y

P
R
O
S
P
E
K
T

Ulitsa Mayakovskogo

Ulitsa Nekrasova

Mytninskaya ulitsa

Novgorodskaya ulitsa

Sinopskaya naberezhnaya

Malookhtinskaya naberezhnaya

Ulitsa Zhukovskogo

37

P
R
O
S
P
E
K
T

PROSPEKT BAKUNINA

38

45

L
I
G
O
V
S
K
Y

P
R
O
S
P
E
K
T

39

Ploshchad
Aleksandra Nevskogo

Key to Map of Leningrad

1. Peter and Paul Fortress
2. Peter the Great's Cottage
3. Cruiser *Aurora*
4. Museum of the 1917 Socialist Revolution
5. Naval Museum (former Stock Exchange)
6. Rostral Columns
7. Kunstkammer
8. Leningrad State University
9. Former Palace of Prince Menshikov
10. Pushkin House
11. Hermitage
12. Alexander Column
13. Admiralty
14. Monument to Peter the Great
15. St. Isaac's Cathedral
16. Astoria Hotel
17. Yevropeiskaya Hotel
18. Summer Garden
19. Peter the Great's Summer Palace
20. Leningrad Branch of the Central Lenin Museum
21. Engineers' Castle
22. Monument to Ivan Krylov
23. Taurida Palace
24. Smolny
25. Monument to Lenin at the Finland Railway Station
26. Russian Museum
27. Ethnographical Museum of the Peoples of the USSR
28. Maly Theatre of Opera and Ballet
29. Theatre of Musical Comedy
30. Shostakovich Philharmonic Society
31. Statue of Alexander Pushkin
32. Kazan Cathedral
33. House of Books (*Dom knigi*)
34. Small Hall of the Shostakovich Philharmonic Society
35. Gostiny Dvor
36. Saltykov-Shchedrin Public Library
37. Palace of Young Pioneers, former Anichkov Palace
38. Moscow Railway Station
39. Alexander Nevsky Lavra
40. Leningrad Conservatoire
41. Kirov Opera and Ballet Theatre
42. Piskaryovskoye Memorial Cemetery
43. Leningrad Hotel
44. Pribaltiiskaya Hotel
45. Moskva Hotel

stone terraces, also by Brenna. In the centre of each stand marble sculptures on granite pedestals. These statues, representing Justice and Peace, were carved in Italy by order of Peter the Great, long before the building of Pavlovsk. All the statues in the park were buried during the Second World War.

Apollo's Colonnade on the left bank of the Slavyanka was built by Cameron in 1780–3, and in the centre is a bronze copy of the Apollo Belvedere. Part of the colonnade collapsed during a flood in 1817, but it was decided to leave the fallen stones to create a more ancient effect. The Pavilion of the Three Graces, a stone terrace with 16 columns supporting the roof, is also by Cameron (1800–01) and the central statue was carved out of a solid block of marble by Trisconni. Cameron's Temple of Friendship on the bank of the river is a graceful domed rotunda in Doric style with sixteen white columns, built in 1780–2.

There is a boating station and an open-air cafe in the park.

Useful Information

Hotels (those with an asterisk belong to Intourist)

Astoria* – 39 *Ulitsa Gertsena*
Baltiiskaya – 57 *Nevsky Prospekt*
Druzhba* – 4 *Ulitsa Chapygina*
Karelia* – 27/2 *Ulitsa Tukhachevskogo*
Kievskaya – 49 *Dnepropetrovskaya ulitsa*
Ladoga – 26 *Prospekt Shaumyana*
Leningrad* – 5/2 *Pirogovskaya naberezhnaya*
Leningradskaya – 10/24 *Prospekt Mayorova*
Mir – 17/19 *Ulitsa Gastello*
Moskovskaya – 43/45 *Ligovsky prospekt*
Moskva* – 2 *Ploshchad Alexandra Nevskogo*
Oktyabrskaya – 10 *Ligovsky prospekt*

Pribaltiiskaya* – 14 *Ulitsa Korablestroitelei*
Pulkovskaya – 1 *Ploshchad Pobedy*
Rossia – 163 *Moskovsky prospekt*
Sovetskaya – 43 *Lermontovsky prospekt*
Sputnik – 34 *Prospekt Morisa Toreza*
Vyborgskaya – 3 *Torzhkovskaya ulitsa*
Yevropeiskaya* – 1/7 *Ulitsa Brodskogo*
Zarya – 40 *Kurskaya ulitsa*

Camping

Olgino* – 18th km of *Primorskoye shosse*
Repino – 9 *Klenovaya ulitsa, posyolok Repino* (Repino settlement), *Leningradskaya oblast* (Leningrad Region)

Museums and Exhibitions

Vladimir Lenin Flat-Museum in Smolny – *Ploshchad Proletarskoy diktatury*, Smolny
Vladimir Lenin Flat-Museum – 7/4 *Pereulok Ilyicha*
Vladimir Lenin Flat-Museum – 52 *Ulitsa Lenina*
Vladimir Lenin Flat-Museum – 17 *Desyataya Sovetskaya ulitsa*
Vladimir Lenin Flat-Museum – 1/106 *Serdobolskaya ulitsa*
Vladimir Lenin Flat-Museum – 32/1 *Naberezhnaya reki Karpovki*
Vladimir Lenin Flat-Museum – 5/7 *Khersonskaya ulitsa*
Sergei Kirov Museum – 26/28 *Kirovsky prospekt*
Museum of the History of Leningrad – 44 *Naberezhnaya Krasnogo Flota*
Museum of the Arctic and Antarctic Research – 24-a *Ulitsa Marata*

Alexander Pushkin Flat-Museum – 12 *Naberezhnaya reki Moiki*

Fyodor Dostoyevsky Literary Memorial Museum – 5/2 *Kuznechny pereulok*

Nikolai Nekrasov Flat-Museum – 36 *Liteiny prospekt*

Nikolai Rimsky-Korsakov Flat-Museum – 28 *Zagorodny prospekt*

Theatrical Museum – 6-a *Ploshchad Ostrovskogo*

Museum of Musical Instruments – 5 *Isaakievskaya ploshchad*

USSR Academy of Arts Museum – 17 *Universitetskaya naberezhnaya*

Writers' Tombs at Volkovo Cemetery – 30 *Rasstannaya ulitsa*

Planetarium – 1 *Park Lenina*

Exhibition Hall of the Artists' Union of the RSFSR – 6 *Bolsheokhtinsky prospekt*

Exhibition Hall of the Leningrad Branch of the Artists' Union of the RSFSR – 38 *ulitsa Gertsena*

Exhibition of Children's Books – 6 *Naberezhnaya Kutuzova*

Industrial Exhibition – 58 *Nevsky prospekt*

Theatres, Concert-Halls and The Circus

Kirov Ballet and Opera Theatre – 1 *Teatralnaya ploshchad*

Maly Opera and Ballet Theatre – 1 *Ploshchad Iskusstv*

Comedy Theatre – 56 *Nevsky prospekt*

Pushkin Drama Theatre – 2 *Ploshchad Ostrovskogo*

Gorky Bolshoi Drama Theatre – 65 *Naberezhnaya reki Fontanki*

Komissarzhevskaya Drama Theatre – 19 *Ulitsa Rakova*

The Lenin Komsomol Theatre – 4 *Park Lenina*
Lensoviet Theatre – 12 *Vladimirsky prospekt*
Theatre of Musical Comedy – 13 *Ulitsa Rakova*
Theatre of Drama and Comedy – 51 *Liteiny prospekt*
Maly Drama Theatre – 18 *Ulitsa Rubinshteina*
Children's Theatre – 1 *Pionerskaya ploshchad*
Variety Theatre – 27 *Ulitsa Zhelyabova*
Puppet Theatre – 52 *Nevsky prospekt*
Bolshoi Puppet Theatre – 10 *Ulitsa Nekrasova*
Shostakovich Philharmonic Society, Large Hall – 2 *Ulitsa Brodskogo;* **Small Hall** – 30 *Nevsky prospekt*
Glinka Choir – 20 *Nabereznaya reki Moiki*
Conservatoire Opera Studio – 3 *Teatralnaya ploshchad*
Oktyabrsky Concert-Hall – 6 *Ligovsky prospekt*
Leningrad Concert-Hall – 1 *Ploshchad Lenina*
Circus – 3 *Naberezhnaya reki Fontanki*

Restaurants

Astoria – 39 *Ulitsa Gertsena*
Baku (Azerbaijan cuisine) – 12 *Sadovaya ulitsa*
Fregat (17th-century Russian cooking) – 39/14 *Bolshoi prospekt*
Kavkazsky – 25 *Nevsky prospekt*
Leningrad – 5/2 *Pirogovskaya naberezhnaya*
Metropol – 22 *Sadovaya ulitsa*
Moskva – 49 *Nevsky prospekt*
Pribaltiisky – 14 *Ulitsa Korablestroitelei*
Sadko (Russian cuisine) – 1/7 *Ulitsa Brodskogo*
Visla (Russian and Polish cuisine) – 17 *Ulitsa Dzerzhinskogo*
Yevropeisky – 1/7 *Ulitsa Brodskogo*

Large Stores

Gostiny Dvor – 35 *Nevsky prospekt*
Dom Leningradskoi Torgovli – 21–23 *Ulitsa Zhelyabova*
Passazh – 48 *Nevsky prospekt*
Frunzensky Department Store – 60 *Moskovsky prospekt*
Kirovsky Department Store – 9 *Ploshchad Stachek*
Souvenirs – 25 *Nevsky prospekt*
Yakhont (jewellery) – 24 *Ulitsa Gertsena*
Agat (jewellery) – 47 *Sadovaya ulitsa*
Chinaware and cut glass – 92 *Bolshoi prospekt*
Cameras, photo equipment – 92 *Nevsky prospekt*
Art Salon – 8 and 45 *Nevsky prospekt*
Dom Knigi (books) – 28 *Nevsky prospekt*
Mir (books from socialist countries) – 13 *Nevsky prospekt*
Leningrad – 50 *Nevsky prospekt*
Krasnaya Shapochka (toys) – 32 *Sadovaya ulitsa*

Major Sports Grounds

Yubileiny Palace of Sports – 18 *Prospekt Dobrolyubova*
Palace of Sports Games – 9 *Ulitsa Butlerova*
Kirov Stadium – 35 *Morskoi prospekt*
Lenin Stadium – 2-g *Petrovsky ostrov*
Tennis courts – 33 *Naberezhnaya reki Fontanki*
Physical Education Centre – 1-3 *Ulitsa Sofii Perovskoy*
Winter Stadium – 6 *Manezhnaya ploshchad*
Large Sports Arena – *Moskovsky park Pobedy*

Leningrad Branch of Intourist Offices – 11 *Isaakyevskaya ploshchad*

17. Artists overlooking Andreyevsky Hill

18. St Sophia's Cathedral and the City

20. Fountains on Kiev Square

22. St Andrew's Church

KIEV

Day 1 – *The Lavra, (Monastery of the Caves), city tour, Botanical Garden and Vydubetsky Monastery, Shevchenko Opera and Ballet Theatre*

Day 2 – *St. Sophia's, Bogdan Khmelnitsky Statue, The Golden Gate, St. Vladimir's Cathedral, Folk Architecture Museum*

Day 3 – *St. Andrew's Church, St Vladimir's Statue, the parks above the Dnieper and the Ukrainian World War II Museum and Memorial, the Historical Museum or one of the art museums, St. Kyril's Church, Babi Yar*

Day 1

**Monastery of the Caves
The Monastery of the Caves (Pecherskaya Lavra, called from the word 'peshchera' meaning 'cave') – Sichneve Povstannya Street 21. Open 9.30–6; closed Tues. The Further Caves are only open from 12–5 and the Nearer Caves are at present closed to the public.

Every visitor to Kiev should certainly try to see this monastery, described as the place

139

Where the darkness of the silent caves
Is livelier than the royal halls.

It was founded in 1051 by two monks, Antony and Theodosius, and through the centuries underground churches were built. In some cases the caves were natural and then the monks themselves excavated further. Some of the members of the community lived their lives there underground and when they died their bodies remained in the cells. Due to the temperature and the chemical properties of the soil, the bodies became mummified and they are still to be seen. 'The whole Orthodox world bows before the relics of the saints of the monastery; in times past and today, undiminished their blessing emanates upon all who come to their tombs in faith and love.'

From the time of Peter the Great and throughout the 18th and 19th centuries almost all the tsars and tsarinas came to Kiev and made lavish gifts to the Lavra, the other monasteries, and the churches of the city. The monastery became exceedingly wealthy and in the 18th century it owned 13 smaller monasteries, 7 towns, 189 villages and three glass factories.

The entrance gate is surmounted by the Trinity Church, which was built in 1108 and contains frescoes and a wooden iconostasis dating from the 18th century. The walls of the Upper Monastery, built between 1698 and 1701, run from this gateway.

Inside, a little way on from the entrance gate, a much smaller archway on the left leads through to an enclosed corner of the monastery grounds surrounding the 17th century Church of St. Nicholas, built in Ukrainian baroque style, and brought here from its original site over Askold's grave. It now serves as a lecture hall, but its appearance is good; it was restored in 1956–7, right up to its blue, star-bedecked dome.

The five-domed All Saints' Church by another gateway was built in the 17th century by the architect

Aksamitov. The iconostasis dates from the end of the 18th century and the murals from 1906 (restored in 1973). The main court of the Upper Monastery centres around the Cathedral of the Assumption (Uspensky Sobor), built in 1073–89 and blown up during the Second World War, but now being rebuilt. Most of the surrounding houses date from the 18th century. In some of these houses were the printing works of the monastery which printed its first book in 1617 and continued to function until the revolution. The architectural complex of the Upper Monastery is completed by the bell-tower which was built in 1731–45 by the St. Petersburg architect Shedel. At 96.5 m (317 ft), it is the highest bell-tower in Russia. The four tiers of the tower are all decorated with pillars and pilasters and a flight of 374 steps leads to the top. In spite of the fact that the tower was constructed in comparatively recent times, there is nevertheless a legend about its construction. It is supposed to have been built by twelve brothers who are now buried in the caves. During construction the tower sank slowly in the earth, thus obviating the use of ladders or scaffolding. When it was completed it sprang out of the earth in a single night.

The way down to the caves leads past the refectory church which was built in 1893 on the site of an older stone building. It was restored in 1956 and is used as a concert hall while the actual refectory is a Museum of Atheism.

Near the walls of the refectory are the graves of the Cossack leaders Judge Kotchubei and Colonel Iskra, executed in 1708 by Ivan Mazepa because they informed Peter the Great of the Ukrainian Hetman's plan to separate the Ukraine from Russia with the help of Charles XII of Sweden and the Zaporozhye Cossacks. Following Mazepa's own treachery, Peter the Great had their mortal remains transferred from their original graves to holy ground. Mazepa's ambitious plan was defeated the following year when the Russian army won the Battle of Poltava.

A last diversion before going down to the caves is to walk onto a wide stone terrace on the right which has a most impressive view over the wooded slopes, the wide river, the spreading suburbs of Kiev and the countryside beyond.

**The Caves

The Nearer Caves, sometimes referred to as St. Anthony's Caves, contain 73 tombs and 3 underground churches; they are at present closed to the public. In the Further Caves, or St. Theodosius's Caves, there are 3 more churches and 47 tombs. They are quite separate from each other. The Belfry of the Further Caves was built in the 18th century by a serf-architect named Stefan Kovnir who also designed one of the houses in the Upper Monastery.

From 1926 to 1964 the whole territory was opened to the public as a museum, with monks caring for it and acting as guides. On entering the caves visitors were asked to purchase a small candle instead of an admission ticket. Then the monks had to leave. Electric light was installed and the interiors of the caves were painted. The mummified bodies still had their names attached, but many of them were further described on anti-religious plaques. In 1988 these holiest of shrines were returned to the Orthodox Church as part of the millennial celebrations (since the adoption of Christianity by Prince Vladimir in 988). The most famous tomb of all is probably that of the chronicler Nestor who died in 1115.

The Historical Treasures of the Ukraine Museum is housed in the building of the monastery bakery. Open 10–5; closed Tues. The items on display date from the 6th to 19th centuries. There are jewellery and coins from the ancient Scythian settlements on the northern coast of the Black Sea as well as pieces of Greek and Roman origin. Here also is the best collection of coins belonging to Kiev Rus. Next door, in the former printing shop of the Lavra, is the Museum of the History of Ukrainian Books and Printing. Open 10–6; closed Tues. The oldest manuscripts here date from the 12th century. Nearby also is the Ukrainian Folk Art Museum – Open 10–5.45; closed Tues. Here are exhibits of embroidery and other handicrafts of the 16th-20th centuries. The Museum of Theatre, Music and Cinematography (open 10–5.45; closed Tues.) is another rich collection within the old monastery walls.

A little to the north of the monastery stands the early 12th-century Church of the Redeemer in the Birchwood (Tserkov Spasa-na-Berestove). The eastern part dates from 1640–43 and contains frescoes of that time. The older part was formerly a sepulchre for the princes of Kiev and in 1157 Prince Yuri Dolgoruki, who had founded Moscow ten years earlier, was buried here. The grey marble tomb now commemorating him was installed in 1947 to mark Moscow's 800th anniversary. It weighs six tons. The church is open as a museum.

**A Tour of the City

Kiev is unlike most of the ancient cities and towns of Russia in that there are no obvious remains of a kremlin or a fortified citadel. A city tour of Kiev will help to demonstrate the three older sections of the city.

Before visiting the individual sites, take a walk along Kreshchatik starting from Lenin-Komsomol Square, noting the many streets criss-crossing (Kreshchatik) this thoroughfare, the waterfalls in front of the Lenin Monument and the beautiful poplar and lime lined Shevchenko Boulevard at the other end.

**Vydubetsk

Vydubetsky Monastery – Vydubetska Street 11.

The monastery is situated on the higher bank of the river Dnieper, south of the Monastery of the Caves, and on part of the 180 hectares (450 acres) belonging to the Academy of Sciences' Botanical Garden. This architectural complex was founded in 1070–77 by Prince Vsevolod and there is a story attached to its unusual name. After the mass conversion of Kievans to Christianity, the powerful pagan idol, Perun, was thrown into the Dnieper. He was carved out of wood but his head was silver and his beard was gold, and apparently the weight of the metal kept him underwater. For some time his distressed followers ran along the river bank shouting, 'Vydubai, come out of the water, O God!' A mile further down he did in fact rise to the surface but there was much confusion and fighting on the bank as the newly baptised Christians were all for letting him continue his journey downstream. It was from the shouts of 'vydubai' that the whole area was thereafter known as Vydubichi, as was the monastery also.

The complex overlooks Vydubetsky Lake which is used for boating in summer. The road runs uphill beside the walls and turns left at the top to reach the entrance gate. Inside and right across the enclosure, overlooking the lake, is St. Michael's Cathedral (1070–88). Only the western side, which has good frescoes, remained after a landslide in the 15th century but the building has recently been reconstructed – and so has the monastery as well. St. George's Church (1696–1701) is a five-domed masterpiece of Ukrainian architecture. The refectory dates from the beginning of the 18th century and the belfry was built in 1730. Between St. Michael's and St. George's is the grave of Konstantin Ushinsky (1824–70), Russian teacher and educationalist.

**Kiev Opera & Ballet

Shevchenko Opera and Ballet Theatre – Volodimerska Street 50. This building was designed in 1901 by Schretter. It seats 1,650. The company was formed in 1926.

Day 2

**St. Sophia's

St. Sophia's Cathedral (Sofiisky Sobor) – Volodimerska Street 24. Open 10–6, closed Thurs.

The cathedral, founded on the tomb of Dir, was dedicated in 1037 by Yaroslav the Wise in gratitude for the victory he gained on this site (then an open meadow outside the city walls) over the Pechenegi, an invading tribe from the east. It was here that the country's earliest historical chronicles were written and the first library organised.

The design of the cathedral was influenced by St. Sophia in Constantinople, but the Kievan cathedral also contains elements of early wooden architecture. When first built, the cathedral was a large five-aisled building with an open gallery on three sides, and 13 cupolas. The first Metropolitan of Kiev, Illarion, wrote of the cathedral in 1037 that 'this church has roused the astonishment and praise of all people around, and nothing like unto it can be found in the breadth of the land from east to west'.

Interesting mosaics and frescoes are to be seen in the central part of the cathedral and in the main dome. The latter contains a mosaic representation of Christ the All-Ruler, the Pantokrator, not the realistic Christ of the Gospels, but a being very closely akin to the other two members of the Trinity.

The archangels surrounding him are dressed in the costume of the imperial court at Byzantium and hold the symbols of the imperial office, the orb and standard. In the apse of the cathedral is the magnificent Virgin Orans, another symbolic figure in mosaic. She is neither the Queen of Heaven nor the Mother of God, but a symbol of the earthly Church interceding for mankind. Both the figure and the splendid golden background survived the ups and downs of the cathedral so that a legend grew up about the wall's indestructability and the Virgin Orans became an increasingly important object of worship. Below the Virgin Orans are depicted the twelve apostles receiving the eucharist and below them are the Fathers of the Church.

In the cathedral's central aisle is a portrait of the family of Yaroslav the Wise and on the walls of the southern and northern towers are pictures of entertainment and hunting, and battle scenes. In the north-eastern part of the cathedral is a marble tomb where in 1054 Yaroslav the Wise was buried.

The cathedral was partly ruined by Tatars and Mongols and was further damaged while the Poles and Lithuanians were ruling the region. It was restored in 1636 and reconstructed at the beginning of the 18th century when six new domes were added. The iconostasis was installed in 1754 and is the work of local craftsmen. After the unification of the Ukraine and Russia in 1654, it was in the cathedral that the Kievans pledged their oath of loyalty. It was also here that Peter the Great celebrated his victory over the Swedish army in 1709. The accoustics are magnificent and any opportunity of hearing them put to the test is to be recommended.

Of the 18th-century buildings, the most outstanding is the 4-storey bell-tower near the main entrance. It was erected between 1744 and 1752 and is 78 m (256 ft) high. Also of interest is the Zabrovsky Gate, built in 1745 as the main entrance to the

Metropolitan's house. It is decorated with elaborate detail and stucco ornament, but has lost its original proportions as the ground level has risen considerably during the past 200 years. The Metropolitan's House was built at the beginning of the 18th century in the style of Ukrainian baroque. To the south of the cathedral is the refectory, built in 1722–30.

The wall surrounding the cathedral was built in the 1740s.

The Sophia Cathedral is now a museum which also displays the architecture of the other old Russian towns of Novgorod and Chernigov and local archaeological finds. The precincts are kept as an architectural and historical monument.

**Bogdan Khmelnitsky

The Bogdan Khmelnitsky Monument is in the centre of Bogdan Khmelnitsky Square, opposite the St. Sophia's Cathedral and near the spot where the Kievans took their oath of loyalty to Russia in 1654. Bogdan Khmelnitsky (1593–1657) was the Cossack Hetman who freed the Ukraine from the Poles and later subjected it to the Moscow state. The equestrian statue was cast in bronze in St. Petersburg by Mikeshin in 1880 and transported to Kiev where it was erected in 1888. The statue is 10.85 m (36 ft) high and so placed that it can be seen from three different directions. The mace Khmelnitsky holds is a symbol of his power as Hetman and it points to the north, to Moscow.

**Golden Gate

The Golden Gate is in the centre of the town. Said to have been inspired by Constantinople's Golden Gate, it is almost the only reminder of the way the city had to fight for its very existence. For many years there were only ruins here, two parallel walls built in 1037 by Yaroslav the Wise to support the main entrance arch into the earthen-walled city of Kiev. These were incorporated in reconstruction work, and now the arch is again surmounted by the small Church of the Annunciation.

**St. Vladimir's

Volodimersky Sobor (St. Vladimir's Cathedral) – Shevchenko Boulevard 20. This cathedral with seven cupolas was built in Byzantine style in 1863–96 by Beretti and Gernhardt to commemorate the 900th anniversary of Christianity in Russia. Sparro was another architect who was involved with the church later. The completed building shows a diversity of styles which resulted from frequent changes of plan. The original idea was to follow the lines of ancient Russian architecture. It is 49 m (54 yds) long, 28 m (31 yds) wide and 50 m (164 ft) in height. The windows are framed with fine stone ornamentation. The walls bear some interesting murals in imitation of Byzantine style. The decorations were carried out under the supervision of Professor Prakhov, a specialist in the history of art, and include some paintings by famous artists, Vasnetsov and Nesterov among others. Vasnetsov's portrayal of the Virgin and Child breaks right away from the traditional Russian icon interpretation. In the central aisle is a painting called The Christening of Russia, showing Prince Vladimir and Princess Olga and the mass baptism taking place. The paintings were restored after the Second World War. It is worth while attending a service here to hear one of the best church choirs in the Soviet Union.

**Wooden Architecture Museum

Folk Architectural Museum – on outskirts of Kiev, near Pirogova village. Open 10–6; closed Wed. Here on a territory of over 100 hectares (250 acres) is sited a collection of 400 old houses, mills, forges and other structures, brought from all over the Ukraine. They are appropriately equipped and furnished so that the items on display number about 30,000.

Day 3

**St. Andrew's

St. Andrew's Church – Andreyevsky Spusk 33. Open, as a museum, 10–5.30; closed Thurs. This church was built in 1744–53 in baroque style by Rastrelli, renowned court architect of St. Petersburg and master of the baroque. It stands on Andreyevsky Hill, the highest point of old Kiev, overlooking Podol, the river and the plain to the east. The site is said to have been chosen for the erection of a cross by the Apostle Andrew himself, when he first preached the Gospel in Russia.

The church stands on a platform reached by a broad flight of steps. It was built at the command of Peter the Great's religious daughter, Elizaveta. It is outstanding for its perfect proportions as well as for the way in which it makes use of the hilltop upon which it stands. Today the domes are green with gilded trim and the walls decorated with blue and gold. Inside, the iconostasis is interesting; it was made under the guidance of portrait-painter Antropov who was also responsible for the frescoes. The church was restored in 1982 to celebrate the 1500th anniversary of the founding of Kiev.

**The Parks

Kiev is lucky to have a beautiful stretch of natural parkland close to the centre, at the northern end of the main street, Kreshchatik. It runs along the hilly wooded slopes above the river. There are really a number of parks here, but they run into each other imperceptibly.

The most northerly is Volodimerska Girka (Vladimir's Hill) where there is an open air cinema seating 1,500 and the St. Vladimir Monument.

St. Vladimir Monument – this statue of Prince Vladimir was erected in 1853 overlooking the river. He is holding aloft a cross. The statue was cast in bronze by Klodt (famous for his horses on the Anichkov Bridge in Leningrad) after a design by Demut-Malinovsky. Prince Vladimir is shown in the dress of an ancient Russian warrior, standing bareheaded in thanksgiving as he gazes at the water of the Dnieper below where he was instrumental in the mass baptism of his people. The statue is 4.5 m (15 ft) high and weighs about 6 tons. The unusual chapel-like pedestal is covered with cast-iron plates. On the pedestal above the bas-relief depicting the baptism of Rus is the old seal of Kiev. The height of the statue and pedestal together is 20.4 m (67 ft).

At the bottom of Volodimerska Girka is another monument dating from 1802 and commemorating the conversion of Russia to Christianity and sited where the mass baptism took place.

Pionersky (pioneer) Park is reached by a flight of steps from Lenkomsomola Square and contains monuments, a cinema and a concert platform. 1-Travnevy (First of May) Park was laid out in 1747–55 as the tsar's park adjoining the palace. There is a band-stand with 2,000 seats, an open air theatre, amusements and the Cuckoo Restaurant. Radyansky (Soviet) Park, laid out in the 19th century, is opposite the tsar's palace and contains a children's village and a playground.

The last of the parks is called Askold's Grave, and contains the city's principal war memorial at Sichneve Povstannya Street 33. It is one of the most beautiful parts of Kiev. There used to be a wooden church dedicated to St. Nicholas over Askold's tomb, where, according to legend, Askold, Prince of Kiev, was buried in 882. This was moved to the upper part of the Lavra territory. In its place (1909) the architect Melensky built a rotunda which now houses a branch of the History Museum. In the upper part of the park, Park Slavy, near the rotunda, is the Tomb of the Unknown Soldier of the Second World War, and as a memorial there is a 27 m (89 ft) obelisk and an eternal flame. Also here are the names of the Heroes of the Soviet Union, engraved in gold on white marble. A little further along is a memorial complex with a Heroes' Avenue, a collection of armaments including a T-34 tank, aeroplanes and a 'katyusha' rocket launcher, and the Ukrainian World War II Memorial Museum – open 10-5; closed Mon. The memorial complex was completed in 1957. Standing on top of the museum and crowning the memorial is the gigantic 62 m (203 ft) stainless steel female figure bearing a sword and shield and symbolising the Motherland that has dominated the high right bank of the Dnieper since 1981.

A good road runs through the park and lower down, beside the river, runs Park Lane, which is closed to motor traffic on summer evenings when it is usually crowded with pedestrians. In the autumn the local fruit and flower show is held here near the statue of the horticulturist, Michurin. Also on Park Lane is an open air theatre with a seating capacity of 4,000. Its amphitheatre makes use of the 19th century wall of Kiev fortress. Higher up the slope, but still in the park area, runs a good motor road with an excellent view across the river. One can get on to it by driving from Paton Bridge along the embankment road and taking the first large left fork up the hill.

**Historical Museum

Historical Museum – Volodimerska Street 2. Open 10–6; closed Wed. The museum contains over 500,000 exhibits dating from prehistoric times to the present day. Of particular interest are the sections on the Scythians and Kievan Rus. Here are examples of 17th and 20th century fabrics and 16th to 19th century handwork. There are also wood carvings, metal-work, and ceramics on view, all displayed to demonstrate Ukrainian art work. Particularly interesting are the krashenki, intricately painted eggs to be exchanged at Easter time. Some rooms here are reserved for temporary art exhibitions. (A branch of the Historical Museum is also housed in the Monastery of Caves.)

**Oriental and Western Art

Museum of Oriental and Western Art – Repin Street 15. Open 10–6; closed Wed. The collection includes Byzantine paintings of the 6th and 8th centuries; Italian Renaissance art including works by Bellini, Tiepolo and Guardi; Flemish and Dutch art of the 15th to 18th centuries including works by Frans Hals and Rembrandt; and works by Velasquez, Goya, Bouchet and David.

**Russian Art

Museum of Russian Art – Repin Street 11. Open 10–6; closed Thurs. The section of Russian art from the 12th to 17th centuries includes icons of the Novgorod, Moscow, and Stroganov schools. The 18th–19th century section contains works by Byullov, Ivanov, Shishkin and Repin. The first quarter of the 20th century is represented by Vrubel, Serov and Korovin among others. Another section shows Soviet art. There is an interesting collection of 18th–20th century porcelain, glass and crystal, and the very imposing house was once the home of the Tereshchenko family, sugar millionaires from Glukhov.

**Ukrainian Applied Art

Museum of Ukrainian Applied Art – Kirov Street 6. Open 10–6; closed Fri. The museum was built under the supervision of Academician Nikolayev in 1898–1900. It was supposed to resemble an ancient Greek temple and the huge granite steps, over 17 m (19 yds) wide, which lead to the main facade have lions at each side. The six-columned portico in antique style is decorated with a sculptured group called 'The Triumph of Art'. The first section of the museum is devoted to Ukrainian art of the 15th-19th centuries, and the second section to works by Soviet Ukrainian artists.

**St. Kyril's

St. Kyril's Church – Frunze Street 103. Open, as a museum, 10–6; closed Thurs. This church was founded on the northern outskirts of Kiev in 1146 as the main church of St. Kiril's Monastery, itself founded in 1140 by Prince Vsevolod. It has been restored several times and its shape dates from the 18th-century reconstruction by Beretti. The 12th-century frescoes were restored in the 1880s under the direction of Professor A. Prakhov and Vrubel worked under him. Vrubel's murals show the weeping over Christ's coffin, and the iconostasis was painted by him too. His 'Entry to Jerusalem' is through the main arch and up, on the immediate right. Upstairs, in the choir gallery, is the descent of the Holy Spirit upon the Apostles with the white of their clothing appearing in mother-of-pearl colours, just as the glazes Vrubel used on ceramics. Around the Holy Spirit mural there are a number of panels with Old Testament prophets, judges and kings.

**Babi Yar

Baby Yar – Drive out of the centre of the city along Artemov Street towards the television tower; just the other side of the tower, on the left of the main road is a monument, unveiled in 1976 and dedicated to the 'Victims of Fascism – 1941–43'. Babi Yar is the name of the wooded gulley where a little stream flows down into the river Pochaina. It runs back from the road at this point and was the scene of gruesome mass murders during the time of the occupation of Kiev. Now planted with young birches, rowans and firs, and criss-crossed with winding footpaths, its very simplicity and silence are deeply moving.

Useful Information

Hotels (those with an asterisk belong to Intourist)

Bratislava* – 1 *Ulitsa Andreya Malyshko*
Desna* – 46 *Ulitsa Milyutenko*
Dnipro* – 1/2 *Kreshchatik*
Leningradskaya* – 4 *Bulvar Tarasa Shevchenko*
Lybid* – *Ploshchad Pobedy*
Mir – 70 *Prospekt Sorokaletiya Oktyabrya*
Moskva – 4 *Ploshchad Oktyabrskoy Revolyutsii*
Rus* – 4 *Gospitainaya ulitsa*
Slavutich – 1 *Ulitsa Entuziastov*
Teatralnaya – 17 *Ulitsa Lenina*
Ukraina – 5 *Bulvar Tarasa Shevchenko*

Camping

Prolisok* – *Pyrataya proseka, Svyatoshino*

Museums and Exhibitions

Kosoi Kaponir (historical, revolutionary, and architectural monument and museum) – 24-a *Gospitalnaya ulitsa*

KEY TO MAP OF KIEV

1. St. Andrew Church
2. History Museum of the Ukrainian SSR
3. Monument to Prince Vladimir
4. Kiev Branch of the Central Lenin Museum
5. Philharmonic Society
6. Dnipro Hotel
7. Oktyabrsky Palace of Culture
8. Dynamo Stadium
9. Former Mariinsky Palace
10. Askold's Grave
11. Museum of the History of the Second World War
12. Metro Restaurant
13. Tchaikovsky Conservatoire
14. Moskva Hotel
15. Monument to Commemorate the 1917 Socialist Revolution
16. Monument to Bogdan Khmelnitsky
17. St. Sophia Architectural Museum-Preserve
18. Golden Gate
19. Taras Shevchenko Opera and Ballet Theatre
20. Intourist Hotel
21. Lybid Hotel
22. St. Vladimir Cathedral
23. Taras Shevchenko Museum
24. Statue of Lenin
25. Monument to Taras Shevchenko
26. Taras Shevchenko University
27. Museum of Western and Oriental Art
28. Museum of Russian Art
29. Botanical Gardens
30. Monument to Nikolai Shchors

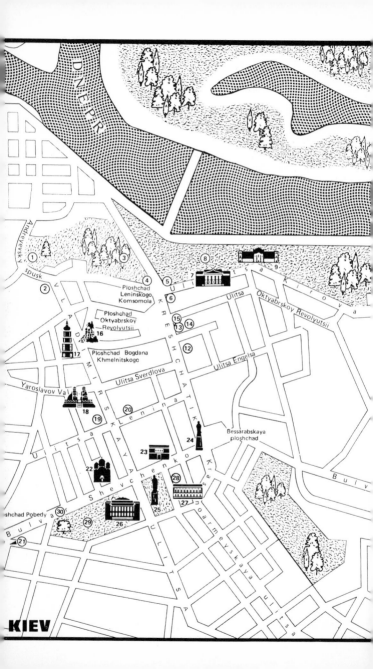

History of Kiev Museum – 8 *Ulitsa Chekistov*
Taras Shevchenko Literary and Memorial House-Museum – 8-a *Pereulok Shevchenko*

Lesya Ukrainka Literary and Memorial Museum – 97 *Ulitsa Saksaganskogo*

Maxim Rylsky Literary and Memorial Museum – 7 *Ulitsa Maksima Rylskogo*

Natural History Museum of the Ukrainian Academy of Sciences – 15 *Ulitsa Lenina*

The Republican Exhibition Hall – 3 *Ultisa Oktyabrskoy Revolyutsii*

Exhibition Hall of the Artists' Union of the Ukrainian SSR – 10/12 *Krasnoarmeiskaya ulitsa*

Artist' Club Exhibition Hall – 1/15 *Ulitsa Artyoma*

Planetarium – 17 *Ulitsa Chelyuskintsev*

St. Cyril Church (12th-18th centuries) – 103 *Ulitsa Frunze*

Vydubitsky Monastery (11th–18th centuries) – *Naddneprovskoye shosse*

Theatres, Concert-Halls and The Circus

Taras Shevchenko Opera and Ballet Theatre – 50 *Vladimirskaya ulitsa*

Theatre of Drama and Comedy – 25 *Prospekt Shestidesyatiletiya Oktyabrya*

Ivan Franko Ukrainian Drama Theatre – 3 *Ploshchad Ivana Franko*

Lesya Ukrainka Russian Drama Theatre – 5 *Ulitsa Lenina*

Operetta Theatre – 51-a *Krasnoarmeiskaya ulitsa*

Children's Theatre – 15–17 *Ulitsa Rozy Luxemburg*

Puppet Theatre – 13 *Ulitsa Shota Rustaveli*

Philharmonic Society – 2 *Vladimirsky Spusk*

House of Organ and Chamber Music – 75 *Ulitsa Krasnoarmeiskaya*

Ukraina Palace of Culture – 103 *Krasnoarmeiskaya ulitsa*
Oktyabrsky Palace of Culture – 1 *Ulitsa Oktyabrskoy Revolyutsii*
Circus – *Ploshchad Pobedy*

Restaurants

Dneprovsky – 14/2 *Bratislavskaya ulitsa*
Dnipro – 1/2 *Kreshchatik*
Dynamo – 3 *Ulitsa Kirova*
Dubki (Ukrainian cuisine) – 1 *Ulitsa Stetsenko*
Intourist – 26 *Ulitsa Lenina*
Kiev – 26/1 *Ulitsa Kirova*
Kureni (Ukrainian cuisine) – *Parkovaya alleya*
Leipzig – 39/24 *Ulitsa Sverdlova*
Leningrad – 4 *Bulvar Tarasa Shevchenko*
Lybid – *Ploshchad Pobedy*
Metro – 19 *Kreshchatik*
Mir – 70 *Prospekt Sorokaletiya Oktyabrya*
Mlyn (Ukrainian cuisine) – *Hydropark*
Moskva – 4 *Ulitsa Oktyabrskoy Revolyutsii*
Myslyvets (Ukrainian cuisine) – *Hydropark*
Natalka (Ukrainian cuisine) – *Kharkovskoye shosse* (18th km)
Prague – *Exhibition of Economic Achievements*
Slavutich – 1 *Ulitsa Entuziastov*
Stolichny – 5 *Kreshchatik*
Teatralny – 17 *Ulitsa Lenina*
Ukraina – 5 *Bulvar Tarasa Shevchenko*
Vitryak (Ukrainian cuisine and decor) – 135 *Prospekt Sorokaletiya Oktyabrya*
Zhokei – 140 *Prospekt Sorokaletiya Oktyabrya*

Large Stores

Ukraina Department Store – *Ploshchad Pobedy*
Central Department Store – 2 *Ulitsa Lenina*
Children's World Department Store – 4 *Ulitsa Zankovetskoy*
Ukrainsky Suvenir (Ukrainian souvenirs) – 23 *Krasnoarmeiskaya ulitsa*
Dom Podarkov (department store) – 5 *Bulvar Lesi Ukrainki*
Perlina (jewelery) –19/21 *Kreshchatik*
Kashtan (jewelery) – 2 *Bulvar Tarasa Shevchenko*
Art Salon – 12 *Ulitsa Lenina*
Dom Muzyki (music shop) – 145 *Krasnoarmeiskaya ulitsa*
Dom Radio (radio goods) – 3 *Bulvar Lesi Ukrainki*
Dynamo (sports shop) – 16 *Bulvar Lesi Ukrainki*
Dom Knigi (bookstore) – 44 *Kreshchatik*
Mistetstvo (books on art) – 26 *Kreshchatik*

Major Sports Grounds and Tourist offices

Palace of Sports – 1 *Sportivnaya ploshchad*
Central Stadium – 55 *Krasnoarmeiskaya ulitsa*
Dynamo Stadium – 3 *Ulitsa Kirova*
Spartak Stadium – 103 *Ulitsa Frunze*
Hippodrome – 140 *Prospekt Sorokaletiya Oktyabrya*
Avangard Cycling Track – 58 *Ulitsa Lenina*

Kiev Branch of Intourist – 26 *Ulitsa Lenina*
Intourbureau (under the City Council for Tourism and Excursions) – 5 *Bulvar Druzhby narodov* (in the Druzhba Hotel)
Kiev Branch of Sputnik Youth Travel Organisation – 4 *Ulitsa Chkalova*